D1565798

The John Pyne Family
in America

Fig 1 The author, Frederick Wallace Pyne, 1991

The John Pyne Family in America

Being the

COMPREHENSIVE GENEALOGICAL RECORD

OF THE DESCENDANTS OF

JOHN PYNE

(1766-1813)

of

CHARLESTON, SOUTH CAROLINA

by

Frederick Wallace Pyne

B.S.C.E., M.S.E.

GATEWAY PRESS, INC.
BALTIMORE   1992

Copies of this book may be ordered
from the author:

Frederick Wallace Pyne
7997 Windsail Court
Frederick, Maryland 21701

Price $20 plus $2 postage and handling

ISBN # 0-9632539-0-5

Library of Congress Catalog Card Number 92-71301

Manufactured in the United States of America
by
GATEWAY PRESS, INC.
BALTIMORE, MARYLAND
FIRST EDITION   1992

DEDICATION

This Study of the History of both the ancestors and the descendants of John Pyne who emigrated from Ireland to Charleston, South Carolina, and biographical information of these interesting persons is dedicated with love and affection to all my children, their descendants, and all other family members, who will hopefully gain some understanding of their background and responsibilities and of the duty to preserve and emulate the good qualities and to sublimate and eliminate the not so good qualities, and thereby become contributing, informed, useful citizens.

TABLE of CONTENTS

LIST of ILLUSTRATIONS

PREFACE

"God's in his heaven:
All's right with the world"
Robert Browning

What is it that inspires one to write about family? Surely it will be felt that few but the most immediate members of the family would be even mildly interested. And just who will it be who really has any concern for this particular bunch? Have they been "movers and shakers", have they been important contributors to the society of their times, does their story provide any clues to the way life was?

Well, some of them might fit those requirements, but mostly they are just solid, "get it done and let the credit go" citizens; responsible people who are, and more who will become, the "backbone" of a nation.

You will find among them business men, bankers, plantation owners, soldiers, sailors, clergymen, teachers, engineers--generally givers of themselves and God's talents. Why then bother with the not inconsiderable effort to find, locate, check, connect, and organize a family genealogy; especially a comprehensive one taking in all the female lines?

It is written because I am the "corporate memory" of the family. Because I now find myself to be the oldest, most senior, living family remainder. Because I am the only "bridge" who can recall the past and the generations who made it. Who else is there who can reach backwards and forwards to 6 or 7 generations? There is none! And to all of the elder statesmen of their respective families, I would say, "Do it while it is still available, or it will be lost".

I owe three debts of gratitude in the preparation of this genealogy. First, to my kinsman Moses Taylor Pyne of Princeton, NJ, (1855-1921), the author of several books on the Pyne family background. One of his statements, that rings so true down through the years, is that no one has a monopoly on knowledge. He was hopeful that his efforts would be followed, in time, by another who would carry-on, correct, add to, and expand his very considerable beginnings. I trust I am that person.

Second, to my grandfather, RADM Frederick Glover Pyne (1879-1962). In an age before the computer, with its tremendous power of data collection and collation, he spent years of laborious (but valuable) time, in writing, seeking, and trying numerous approaches to problems that I am enabled to solve almost at the flick of a finger. His persistance and energy in following small clues must be admired. Moreover, he gave me the interest to pursue the matter. He collected a great deal of primary information.

He sought, but failed to find the connection between his great-great-great grandfather The Rev Cornelius Pyne and the immigrant from Ireland, John Pyne. He knew (or thought he knew) that this was another John Pyne, but could find no dates or connectable information. It was the computer and the research engendered by the "Irish Genealogist", especially that of Dr. Henry F. Morris, that finally unravelled the mystery!

Third, to the dual team of my godson and nephew Philip Schuyler Pyne and to my son Stephen VanRensselaer Pyne, first cousins (but more like brothers), who for their youth, enthusiasm, love of history and family, and their willingness to seek and produce go my eternal thanks! Excursions through South Carolina newspapers, Court Records, Deeds, Census Records, and innumerable other databases unlocked much minute data. Visits, phone calls, and information requests to Libraries, Historical Societies, Hereditary Societies, and family archives released hidden information of great value!

Building, then, upon the bases provided by others and Researching and seeking on my own, I present to the reader this Genealogy of John Pyne, his ancestors and his related descendants in the Adams, Bankhead, Barretto, Braun, Burrill, Cary, Correia, Cowley, Crow, DiGiacomo, Edwards, Guest, Hover, Hutchinson, Kennedy, Lewis, Lundie, March, Marr, Morris, Mulford, Neilson, Newhall, Oliver, Ostrander, Parker, Patterson, Perry, Roberts, Saliba, Shadduck, Schreiber, Smelser, Washburn, Way, and Whitelock lines.

As with my forebears, it is my hope that a future researcher will pick up the gauntlet of genealogy, and carry on the efforts so nobly begun into other generations yet unborn. To that end, space has been left at the end of certain Chapters for the insertion of biographical and genealogical information on pages labelled "NOTES".

7997 Windsail Court
Frederick, Maryland
5 April 1992

Frederick Wallace Pyne, P.E.; F.ASCE

A FAMILY PRAYER

So many family members have been givers: clergymen, servicemen, businessmen, teachers, mothers, and contributors to the communities in which they lived, that it should come as no surprise that when Scouting came along in the early 20th century, Pynes were attracted to it. As a program for Character Development, Citizenship Training, and Fitness it appealed to family members sense of rightness, worthiness, and duty.

The National Council of the Boy Scouts of America has a training and high adventure camp at Philmont, NM. The author and his family have been there many times. If God's purpose for us is to make the best of the talents and abilities and to wisely use the resources He has bestowed upon us, then perhaps the following Grace, which this family uses, may prove helpful to others:

"For food, for raiment,
For life, for opportunity;
For friendship and fellowship,
We thank thee, O Lord." Amen.

Philmont Scout Grace

HOW TO USE THE BOOK

The title of this book may indicate that it is the descendants of John Pyne of Charleston, SC only that are being considered. Not so! In order to provide background, the first four Chapters are devoted to his ancestors. Chapter I reviews the very early beginings of the family. In it will also be found a generation by generation recital of his patrilineal ancestors, identified by capital roman numerals for each generation. Some of this background is also summarized for inclusion in Chapter II, allowing it to stand alone. Chapter III discusses the single Irish Generation in the family. Chapter IV is an overview of what coming to America by sailing ships was like.

Chapters V and VI include the family history and genealogical record of John Pyne (1766-1813) and his children. The remaining seven Chapters discuss the families of his five married children, in the order of birth, down to the present. The male line, descendants of Smith Pyne (1803-1875), requires three chapters (X, XI, XII).

An Appendix contains a list of abbreviations used, and an explanation of the calendar. The Appendix also contains a particularly useful discussion of the lines touched upon in Chapter I. Whereas in that Chapter the ancestors are merely listed, in the Appendix the discussion includes references and more data.

A bibliographic essay is included. This is a valuable mine to explore for those who want more detail on where material may be found and how it was evaluated.

The numbering system used for all of the 177 descendants of John Pyne in the text of this family history is that of the Modified New England Historic and Genealogical Register (NEHGR). Each individual has a number. In addition, a second small roman numeral may appear before a person's name; that is the order of birth. A third number, as a superscript, may appear after a person's name; that is a generational reference.

Where there has been issue or if the person is more fully discussed in the text, a "+" will appear before his number.

Thus we find:

+ 119 iv. David Wallace PYNE^7 (Charles Schuyler Pyne^6, Frederick Cruger Pyne^5, Frederick Glover Pyne^4, Charles March Pyne^3, Smith Pyne^2, John Pyne^1).

This traces David as number 119, in the seventh generation from the founder, John Pyne, and that he is the fourth child in his parents' family. It also tells the reader how and who were the line of descent, and the name of every generation with their respective generational superscript.

Likewise will also be found:

+ 84 i. Jennifer PYNE^6 (John Pyne^5, John Pyne^4, Henry Rogers Pyne^3, Smith Pyne^2, John Pyne^1).

References cited within the text are numbered, enclosed in ( ), and reported at the end of each chapter.

CHAPTER I

IN THE BEGINNING

"It was a mighty while ago"
Ben Jonson

Surnames, as we know them today, did not exist in ancient times. People were known merely by a simple given name. That seemed to be adequate when the world was much less crowded and everyone knew their neighbor. A number of books describe how surnames came into being, usually grouping them into four general classes.

One of these classes of surnames is those which are derived from a place name or the locality of the bearer of such a surname. "Ford" would be someone "from the ford", thus Ashford or Oxford. As early as the middle of the 8th century A.D., a southwestern European family, probably controlling the pine-covered northern slopes of Mont Jou in the Spanish Pyrenees began to use the surname "of the pines" or "of the pine grove", and called themselves de los Pinos or de Pinos (1).

1

The site of the origin of the Pyne family, "the ancient Tribe of Great Reputation of Pyne", is almost certainly the Catalonia-Pyrenees area of the Spanish-French borderlands. We find that a Galceran de los Pinos lived in that vicinity as early as 754 A.D. at the time of King Pepin of France. Another of the same name was appointed to be one of the famous nine Barons of Catalonia ("L'un de la neuf") by King Charlemagne in 810 A.D. (2).

This Galceran received large estates from the King in the province of Catalonia and was the ancestor of the Barons and Marquises de Pinos who bore such titles as Marquis de Barbera, Marquis de Alentorn, Marquis de Castro Pinos, Count of Guimera and of Valfogona, Viscount of Illa, of Evol, of Canet, of Alquerforadat, and Grandee of Spain where the family flourished for more than a thousand years.

Descendants of this Spanish house later settled in France, where we find an E. Pyne of Alderney listed in the Domesday book in 1086, and a French house is found in Aquitaine by 1120. In France the family used the patronymic "de Pins". In the early part of the 20th century this French house was represented by the Marquis de Pins et de Montbrun. The branch of this de Pins line, from which the English family traces its descent, became extinct in the male line in France in the later part of the 19th century.

2

The family of Pyne (occasionally also Pine) was founded in England by Hebert de Pyn (or de Pins) of the French line who came to England with Eleanor of Aquitaine in 1154 at the time of the ascension to the throne of King Henry II. He quickly settled down at Upton in County Devon, as the Lord of the Manor, to which place was given the name Upton Pyne (3).

The Spanish House, the French House, and the English House all bear strikingly similar coats of arms. These are blazoned by the Heralds in the English College of Arms as: "Gules, a chevron ermine between three pine cones erect or." [A red field upon which are three gold colored pine cones, standing upright on their bases, spaced between an ermine colored chevron]. There is no question but that the direct family male lines of this ancient Devonshire family are armigerous and are entitled to have and use a coat of arms.

Fortunately, the somewhat elevated station of the family made its descent comparatively easy to trace. Moses Taylor Pyne was established in his right to bear Arms by Norry King at Arms on 3 Mar 1919, and the author is entitled to, and could confirm, this right for his line through the College of Arms, although its value in this country is somewhat ornamental. The record of the estates, marriages, and lineages of those families entitled to bear Arms were always carefully preserved in Spain, France, and England.

3

While there are other families with the same patronymic who came to England in the wake of William the Conqueror in and after 1066, most of them appear to have settled in the area north of the River Trent. It is, however, the branch of the family that settled in the west of England that is the special interest of this Family History.

From the Herbert de Pyn, who came to England in 1154 and who was witness to a grant circa 1160 and died before 1166, we trace the direct male line down in unbroken sequence for 27 generations to the author. Both Burke's "Landed Gentry", 1952 (4) and Burke's "American Families with British Ancestry", 1939 (5) are needed in order to follow the pedigree. It is not the author's purpose to redo these matters, but to report to interested readers the fact of their existence, and to summarize herein the ancestry of the John Pyne in the title of this book.

I   Upon the death of Herbert de Pyn, Patriarch, in 1166, the founder of the English line who had four sons, we trace the direct male line of descent as follows:

II   Sir Simon de Pyn of Upton Pyne, son of Herbert, the patriarch. Note that at this early period (1166), long before the College of Arms was created and was making Visitations (the method of confirming a right to Arms), which commenced in 1530 and came to an end in 1687, we find a Pyne holding a Knights fee (a feudal duty) in Devon and bearing the traditional arms of the Pyne Family.

4

III   Sir Herbert de Pyn II of Upton Pyne, son of Sir Simon. He was probably with King John's principal advisor William, Lord Briwer at the signing of the Magna Carta in 1215, since he owed feudal duties to William and would have been called upon to guard him during such an important and potentially dangerous undertaking.

IV   Sir Herbert de Pyn III of Upton Pyne, son of Herbert, succeeded him as Lord of the Manors of Upton Pyne, Bramford Pyne, Washford Pyne, Colum Pyne, and other fees in Devon and Cornwall about April 1219. He was appointed Justice of Assize by King Henry III on 20 Aug 1223.

V   Simon de Pyn II, son of Sir Herbert de Pyne III, held these fees for a short period (c. 1250-1264).

VI   Sir Herbert de Pyn IV, of Upton Pyne, son of Simon, was presented as patron to the Church of Upton Pyne on 12 Oct 1264. The Feudal Aid Books tell us that he is reported as holding ten fees directly of King Edward I in 1293. The King summoned him to perform military service in person against the Scots in 1301, which he did, resulting in the capture of Stirling Castle. He is reported to have died early in 1309, leaving a son John.

VII   John de Pyn, of Upton Pyne, son of Sir Herbert was a member of Parliament in 1335. He appears in the Writs of Parliament as John de Pyn, Armiger, which meant that he had entitlement to bear arms. He died in 1336.

VIII   Sir Thomas de Pyne, Knighted by King Edward III in 1328, son of John, was returned in 1337 as holding the Cornish fees of his father. Note that the spelling now adds the "e" to the surname. Thomas was the eldest of John's two sons and succeeded to Washford Pyne and the Cornish fees previously noted, while the younger son, William, inherited Upton Pyne. Thomas left two sons upon his death circa 1363.

IX   Oliver Pyne, Armiger, the eldest son of Sir Thomas. Notice that now we also find that the Norman-French "de" is dropped from the surname. In this ninth generation following Herbert de Pyn, Oliver Pyne married Ellinor de Downe in 1396 and settled in the manor of East Down, which became the principal seat of that branch of the Pyne family traced in this history (Fig 2). This Manor is located about midway between Barnstable and Lynton in north Devonshire. Many members of this line were Clergymen or Gentlemen Planters. They were all learned persons and prominent among the landed gentry of Devon and Cornwall, where they owned much property, and had entitlement to coat armour.

6

Fig 2 View of the Manor House at East Down

Many members who had entered upon Holy Orders became Rectors of the Church at East Down and many Pynes are buried there, at the Church of St. John the Baptist (Fig 3). Albeit tracts of land from the original estate and village had been off-conveyed from the property over the years, family members occupied the Manor House of East Down as recently as 1939. It is currently owned by others.

Fig 3 View of the Church of St. John the Baptist at East Down.
Note the War Memorial.

8

Oliver Pyne and Ellinor de Downe had issue, and the male line continues to descend as follows:

X Robert Pyne of East Down, son of Oliver Pyne. He held in 1428, in addition to the Manor of East Down, the manors of Ham in Morwenstow, Bere, Alwington, Westovy, and Marhamchurch, being the ten fees which his grandfather Thomas de Pyne and his great-great grandfather Sir Herbert de Pyn IV had formerly held.

XI John Pyne of East Down, son of Robert, held numerous fees and manors in both Devon and Cornwall. He died in 1483, leaving two sons and a daughter.

XII Nicholas Pyne of East Down, eldest son of John, married Thomazine Winslade by whom he had a daughter and two sons. He died 23 Apr 1510. It is interesting to note that his younger brother, Thomas, became holder of the Manor of East Lyn and is referred to as Thomas Pyne of Lynton. Thus the family influence in the northern part of Devonshire was widely spread.

XIII George Pyne of East Down, second son of Nicholas Pyne inherited the Manor of East Down and other Devon estates, while the Cornish fees went to his elder brother Thomas. George died 20 Jul 1530.

XIV   Nicholas Pyne of East Down, eldest of three sons of George and Isabel Pyne, was born in 1509. He and his wife Elizabeth Chichester had one son, John, and several daughters. Nicholas owned much land in Devon. In 1564 the College of Arms confirmed to him the ancient arms of the Pyne family. He died in 1574.

XV   John Pyne of East Down, son of Nicholas, for whom a pedigree was recorded in 1564 (6), died in 1572, before his father, but left a large family of six sons and four daughters. He married, at East Down, Honor Penfound on 10 Jul 1554. (See Appendix, pp 177-180 for a referenced discusssion of the descent from 1154 to 1564)

XVI   John Pyne (1564-1616), the fourth son of John Pyne and Honor Penfound, was admitted to Holy Orders in 1587 and became the Rector of East Down. He had two daughters and two sons.

XVII   Josias Pyne, second son of The Rev John Pyne of East Down was baptized on 29 Nov 1604. Josias married Christian Heydon on 21 Jun 1616 at Arlington Parish Church, near East Down. They had a son, Philip.

XVIII Philip Pyne, only son of Josias and Christian
Pyne was baptized 2 Feb 1626/27 at Arlington. He
was a ninth generation descendant of Oliver Pyne,
and eighteenth in descent from the patriarch, and
married (1st) Anne Oxenham on 12 Nov 1644. She
died in 1668.

In Chancery Proceedings this Philip Pyne is referred to as
"Gentleman", meaning that he had entitlements to dignity and arms.
Philip and Anne Pyne had five children, the youngest of whom was
John Pyne. Although East Down was the principal seat of the Pyne
family for several centuries, not every member lived there, but
moved or were called by profession to other places. This was true
of a descendant of Oliver Pyne of East Down, John Pyne, son of
Philip Pyne.

XIX John Pyne, born in 1655 and baptised on 30 May
1655 at West Down, matriculated at Exeter
College, Oxford, and graduated B.A. in 1676. He
was called to be the Vicar of Yarnescombe in
1677.

Thus, a 19th generation descendant of the original
English west country Patriarch, Herbert de Pyn, a member of a
family long associated with East Down, Devon, relocated to
Yarnescombe, another part of this same county where he died in
1723 (7).

This John Pyne (XIX) of Yarnescombe, Devon, England had issue. His fourth child, Cornelius Pyne, was sent to Trinity College in Dublin, Ireland in 1708. A grandson of this Cornelius emigrated to America one hundred years later, in 1808, and it is he who is the progenitor of that branch of the Pyne family in America today! Finding him, and the missing generation in-between, and then following his progeny through all the subsequent generations to the present time has been the focus of this family history.

(1) "Descendants of Galceran de Pinos" New York 1915
(2) "Memorials of the Pyne Family" Princeton 1919
(3) Ibid
(4) Landed Gentry of Great Britian, 1952
(5) American Families with British Ancestry 1939
(6) College of Arms D7 73
(7) Yarnescombe Parish Records

NOTES

CHAPTER II

THE   ENGLISH   FOUNDATION

"The boast of heraldry, the pomp of pow'r,
And all that beauty, all that wealth e'er gave,
Awaits alike the inevitable hour:
The paths of glory lead but to the grave."

Thomas Gray

It has been well established that Herbert de Pyn (I) became Lord of the Manor at Upton Pyne, living there before 1160 (1). Moses Taylor Pyne, in his extensive works on the family published in 1915 and 1919 (2),(3) states that the ancestry of the Pyne family can be traced back in the direct male line to this Herbert de Pyn (or Pyne or Pins). He further points out, that this de Pins bears the same arms as the Guillaume Raymond de Pins living in Aquitaine, head of the French House before 1154. This was the year in which Henry II and his wife, Eleanor of Aquitaine, went to England to receive the English Crown. It was expected that the head of important families, or a kinsman thereof, would be supplied to attend her. It is with undoubted certainty that the de Pins kinsman of her retinue was this same Herbert de Pyn (de Pins) of whom we treat.

15

This first Herbert De Pyn was the progenitor and patriarch of the family in the west of England. His progeny held numerous fees of land in Devon and Cornwall in addition to Upton Pyne, including: Washford Pyne, Morwenstow, Ham, Monkoakhampton, Chelfham, Launceston Castle, Alwington, Marhamchurch, Bere, Colum Pyne, Bramford Pyne, and East Down. Sir Herbert de Pyne IV (5th generation from the progenitor) was summoned during the reign of Edward I in 1301 to fight the Scots. His son, Thomas de Pyne, was knighted by Edward III in 1328, and it was his grandson, Oliver Pyne (IX), who married Ellinor de Downe in 1396 and thus became the founder of the Pynes of East Down.

This Oliver Pyne's great-great-great grandson, Nicholas Pyne (XIV), b. 1509, married Elizabeth Chichester. In 1564 the College of Arms confirmed to him and to his son John the ancient arms of the Pyne family (Fig 4). This son, John Pyne (XV) was married in 1554 to Honor Penfound. A more detailed Generational Table than the list found in the previous Chapter from the progenitor Herbert de Pyn to this John Pyne is given in the Appendix.

The Rev John Pyne (bap 1564), the 4th son of John Pyne (XV), was Rector of East Down and 16th in descent from the progenitor, Herbert de Pyn. A reprint of the Harleian MSS 1163-1164, "The Visitation of the County of Devon in the Year 1620", shows this family line from Nicholas to John Pyne (4).

16

Fig 4   Shield of the Pyne Coat of Arms
Gules, a chevron ermine, between three pine cones erect or

17

The Rev John Pyne's grandson, Philip Pyne married (1st) Anne Oxenham in 1644. By her, he had five children, including three sons, the youngest of whom was John Pyne (5). This younger John Pyne took Holy Orders and became the Vicar of Yarnescombe in 1677. He married Joan Hunt of Tavistock in 1682 and had issue.

The Rev John PYNE (XIX) of Yarnescombe, County Devon, England, was born in Devon, England in 1655, and baptized at West Down on 30 May 1655. He entered Exeter College, Oxford on 12 March 1673 and graduated B.A. 10 Oct 1676 (6). He was Ordained in 1677 and became the Vicar of Yarnescombe that same year, a position he held until his death in May 1723. He married Joan Hunt of Tavistock on 7 February 1681/2 (she died in November 1712). They are both buried in the churchyard in Yarnescombe (7). In 1696 he and his wife leased some gardens and 52 acres of land in West Hollock, Colehouse at Huggle Down in Yarnescombe to Walter Jollow for their lifetimes at the rate of 10 shillings a year (8).

He must have been moderately well off since his creditors claim that he was the possessor of an estate with an annual income of £40 in addition to his living as the Vicar of Yarnescombe worth an additional £40 annually or more (9). Issue of the Rev John Pyne and Joan Hunt Pyne:

   i. Eusebius PYNE   bp. 21 Sep 1682 d. 1721
   ii. John PYNE   bp. 7 Apr 1684 d. 1752
   iii. Philip PYNE   bp. 11 Sep 1687 m. 1722 d. 1752
+ iv. Cornelius PYNE bp. 10 Nov 1689 d. 1749
   v. Mary PYNE   d. 1722

The Rev Cornelius PYNE (XX), 4th son of the Rev John Pyne, was probably born in the spring of 1689. Although the Baptismal Record of the Church at Yarnescombe seems to indicate a date of 10 Nov 1687, that must be seen as a misinterpretation of the writing, because he was not likely to have been baptized only two months after his brother Philip. We believe he was Baptized at Yarnescombe on 10 Nov 1689, since he entered Trinity College, Dublin, Ireland on 2 Jun 1708 at the age of 19, and must, therefore, have been born between late Jun 1688 and May 1689 (10).

He was a scholar in 1711, B.A. in 1712, and M.A. in 1715. He was Ordained a Deacon that year and Priested by the Bishop of Cloyne on 23 Sep 1716. Like his father, he was a lifelong Vicar of a country parish church--Cornelius's being at Kilworth, County Cork, Ireland, where he served from 1719 to 1749. While the old church building is still there (Fig 5), it was made redundant, sometime between the disestablishment in 1869 and WWII, and is now in the hands of the Roman Catholic Diocese and is being used as an arts and crafts center.

This old Parish Church Building served the local community in and around the Kilworth area, including the Manor House and grounds of nearby Ballinacarriga about a mile away.

Fig 5 Parish Church at Kilworth

Cornelius died there sometime before 3 June in 1749 (11), serving at his parish church in Kilworth. Rather late in life (at the age of nearly 43), on 6 May 1732, he married Margaret Markham, widow of Hugh Crosse. They had a son, their only child:

+ i John PYNE b. c. 1735 d. 1812 of whom we treat, in the next Chapter.

(1) Burkes Landed Gentry, 1952
(2) Galceran de Pinos, M.T. Pyne, 1915
(3) Memorials of the Pyne Family, Vol I, 1919
(4) "The Visitation of the County of Devon in the Year 1620"; 1872
(5) The Irish Genealogist, Part IV, 1987, Vol 7 #2
(6) Alumni Oxonsienses, Foster
(7) The Irish Genealogist, Part IV p.235, 1987
(8) Feet of Fines 8 William III, Trinity Term Bundle 823
(9) Chancery proceedings, Whittington, 446 Marshall vs. Pyne
(10)Trinity Alumni, Dublin
(11)The Irish Genealogist, Part IV p.236, 1987

CHAPTER III

THE IRISH TRANSITION

"Winding up days with toil
and nights with sleep"

William Shakespeare

John PYNE (XXI) of Kilworth, only child and son of the Reverend Cornelius Pyne and Margaret Markham Pyne, was born circa 1735. The exact date and place of birth are now lost because the church records were destroyed by a fire during the "troubles" in Ireland during 1922, after their submission to Dublin. However, since his father was Vicar of Kilworth, and his mother had been assigned the lands of Ballinacarriga, in the parish, under the marriage settlement, it is almost certain the boy was born and Baptized there.

He is reported to have been "carefully educated and possessing good abilities but neglecting Minerva and the Muses, he cultivated the God Bacchus with zealous energy". Just where or what this "careful education" was has not been discovered. It apparently was not at his father's school, Trinity College, since the records of that institution reveal no such person as having attended.

21

The records at Eton and Oxford, where other family members went, have also been checked without results. He surely must have enjoyed his drink, although that was not uncommon in his day, but to be remembered for that indulgence suggests that he was a bit of a lush.

We experienced the greatest difficulty in trying to find and pin down this John Pyne. The author's grandfather, RADM Frederick Glover Pyne, had spent many, many years in letter writing and searching in order to obtain some information relating to the son of Cornelius Pyne, all without definitive results. It was a serendipitous piece of good fortune that led the author, through a distant English relative, to a full discussion of this part of the family, as reported in the "Irish Genealogist" (1). (See also the Bibliography p. 190).

John Pyne married Isabella Pyne, daugher of Henry Pyne (Wakeham) and Mary Strait in 1757 (2). Isabella died 27 October 1809, aged 66, and is buried in the churchyard at Kilworth. John died in County Cork, and his will proved in Cloyne in 1812. John Pyne and Isabella Pyne had issue:

  i. Cornelius PYNE m. 1790 d. 1803
+ ii. John PYNE (XXII) b. 1766 d. 1813
   of whom we treat in the next Chapter
  iii. Richard Markham PYNEb. 1772 d. 1805
  iv. Margaret PYNE m. 1791
  v. Isabella PYNE b. 1781 d. 1803

This John Pyne (XXI) was the only full generation with the Pyne patronomyic in the line being discussed to have been born and to have died on Irish soil. His forebears had come from England, specifically from East Down, County Devon, via Yarnescombe. His descendant line, through his second son John Pyne (XXII), emigrated to the United States and remains there to this day. Thus he was the Irish transition to America from England.

(1) Irish Genealogist, part iv, 1987, pp235-239
(2) Cloyne Marriage License Bonds

NOTES

CHAPTER IV

COMING TO AMERICA

"...the way of a ship in the midst of the sea..."
                                    Proverbs XXX, 19

We have all read about the three little cockleshells in which Columbus and his crew sailed on the "Enterprise of the Indies" a half a thousand years ago. The trip of the Pilgrims in 1620 and of the great Puritan migrations of 1630-1640 are also well documented. Very many crossings of the Atlantic Ocean were made in the 17th and 18th centuries, during and after the period of the American Revolution, and on into the first quarter of the 19th century before the coming of steamships.

Travelling across an ocean in a non-sail powered vessel is quite a different thing than using natural wind power as the means of propulsion. All of the millions of immigrants who came through Ellis Island came by mechanically-powered steamboat or packet. Their passage has been much discussed; it was not comfortable, pleasant, or enjoyable. Yet by comparision with those who had come before on a sail-powered vessel, it was a lark!

25

This chapter seems a good place in which to describe a sea crossing by sail, not only because it is not done anymore (except by specialists), but because a knowledge of the many difficulties, discomforts, horrors, and hazards involved in such an endeavor may be central to an understanding of our ancestors' grit, courage, and determination.

If your ancestor came to America, across the Atlantic, anytime between the settlement at Jamestown in 1607 to about the 1820's, he came in a sailing vessel! Oh, yes indeed, he may have come over in a sailing craft at some period after that, but it becomes increasingly unlikely as the century progresses.

Sailing across the Atlantic during the 300 year period from the age of discovery until the coming of steam power did not change in greatly significant ways. True, there had been some improvements. Vessels were generally somewhat larger, and ship design was better and more stable. John Harrison of England had developed the chronometer that allowed quite accurate determination of longitude. The sextant also came into use, replacing the more cumbersome quadrant, so that latitude could be much more accurately determined.

It follows that charts were, therefore, much more accurate. Something was known about sea currents and winds, although the very detailed mapping of these important aspects of sailing and sea navigation would await the work of LT Matthew Fontaine Maury in the 1830's. Scheduled packets did not come into use until just before 1820, and the "sharp" design of the clipper ships didn't emerge until the 1840's. So in 1800 we still had broad-beamed, slow (average speed 4 knots), relatively small merchant ships, and they were sailing ships.

Size of shipping in those earlier days was not rated, as we do today, by tons of water displaced by the weight, shape, and draft of a ship, which we call "displacement". Rather, the measure of a vessel's size was its capacity to carry goods. Our forebears were much less interested in how large or heavy a ship was; what was of interest was how much she could carry! This capacity was measured by the number of "tuns" (or the equivalent cubic capacity) that could be stored in its cargo hold. A "tun" was a great, huge, quadruple, hogshead or double butt of 252 gallons! The Mayflower was a ship of about 100 tuns.

The great ship design changes that came after 1820, particularly the "Clipper Ships" of the 1840's, were competing against the growing reliability and dependability of steam-powered vessels. These new "sharp" sailors offered speed, whereas steam offered freedom from the vagaries of the wind. Ordinary shipping craft in the first decade of the 19th century, however, were still small and uncomfortable, and totally dependant upon wind, current, and weather.

We do not know from which port our John Pyne immigrant sailed, nor do we know the name of the vessel, or the route across. But we can make some intelligent surmises, which will help us describe the event.

The vessel was most likely a ship, schooner, brig, or bark. It is the manner of rigging and the number of masts and sails that determine a vessel's type. Lanteen rigging, so useful in the narrow seas of the Near East, is not totally satisfactory in the wide waters and the following winds of the oceans. That means that the vessel was most probably ship rigged.

The ship must also have been basically a cargo vessel, a merchant ship, occassionaly taking passengers as supercargo. Its size might have been about 250-300 tuns. A few small spaces on the 'tween decks, normally used for cargo, may have been converted to cabin space for paying gentlemen passengers.

Considering the command of the seas that England enjoyed at that time, this ship was probably British. Her home port may have been Portsmouth, Liverpool, London, or Bristol, but she trans-shipped across the Irish Sea to Dublin, Wexford, Waterford, Cork, or perhaps even the western Irish ports of Limerick or Galway.

John Pyne stated in his application for U.S. Citizenship that he had arrived in Charleston on 28 Feb 1808. In the absence of any other data, and knowing of no reason why this date would be improper, we must accept it as correct.

28

Working backwards we can imagine a time shortly before Christmas 1807 when John Pyne comes either from Ballinacarriga, near Kilworth, or Nenagh to the Port of Cork. There the family, with some servants, settled into two small cabins, stocked in food and drink (the ship provided no such thing as service in those days), and lived aboard for a few weeks awaiting final lading, wind, and tide (1).

Crossing times naturally varied a great deal, but a majority of shippings would fall within a period of 3-8 weeks, including the sometimes needed side trips. This ship weighs anchor on 14 Jan 1808 and slips out of the harbor on the outgoing morning tide, with a fair wind on the starboard quarter, bound for the Azores, the West Indies, and Charleston. This southern route was the most common, and in the long run, quickest, way across in the days of sail. One did not normally buck the North Atlantic, especially in the winter, unless heading for such northerly ports as St. John's or Halifax, in Nova Scotia.

While the ocean can be calm, and can seem both powerful and beautiful, it can also be troublesome. John Pyne and his family would then be subjected to the fierce storms, calms, sickness, stench, uncertainties, quiet, boredom, fear, death, poor food, disgusting water, and crowding (2) of an Atlantic crossing by sail. After stops for fresh water and provender at the Azores and St. Croix, and 46 days at sea, our patriarch finally arrives at the Port of Charleston, SC on 28 Feb 1808.

(1) Men, Ships, and the Sea; NGS, p. 214
(2) Voyagers to the West, B. Bailyn, pp320-322

CHAPTER V

THE IMMIGRANT
THE FIRST GENERATION

"We are ready to try our fortunes"
William Shakespeare

Thomas Pyne came to New York in 1828. He was the grandfather of Moses Taylor Pyne, author of earlier Family Histories (see Bibliography pp. 193-194). Thomas was also a descendant of John Pyne (XV) and Honor Penfound of East Down through their third son, George Pyne. There were much earlier Pynes who had come both to New England and to Virginia, who do not seem to be related to the Pynes of East Down or of Upton Pyne, but come from the more easterly counties of England. We find, for example, that an Arthur Pyne, a cordwainer of London, has a daughter, Hannah Johnson, living in Accomack, VA in Sep 1655. A John Taylor of Bristol was apprenticed to John Pyne of Virginia on 30 Sep 1667. A Matthew Pyne sailed on the "Pine Tree" from Exeter to New England between 9 Feb and 8 Mar 1683. There are others. But it is the one who came to Charleston, SC in 1808 that concerns us.

+1 John PYNE[1], (XXII) the second son of John Pyne (XXI) of Kilworth and Isabella Pyne was born in Nenagh, County Tipperary, Ireland on 14 February 1766. In 1782, at 16 years of age he was apprenticed to John Cole, Jr (1).

31

A search of the records at Trinity College, Eton College, and Oxford University, all of the most likely places for this individual to have taken a formal education, yield no information that he matriculated at any of them. We must conclude that his education was home, local, and family centered.

It is to be noted that his grandmother, Margaret Markham Pyne, gave £50 in trust, the income to be used annually to teach poor scholars to read. A tablet memorializing this gift is found in the parish church at Tavistock (2). He married circa 1789 Honora Smith (b.1765), daughter of O'Brien Smith and Margaret Parsons.

Margaret Parsons' brother, James Parsons, had come to America well before the Revolution. On 11 May 1750 he was admitted to the South Carolina Court of Common Pleas. He was one of the leaders in the patriot cause. He was a member of the Council of Safety for St. Michael's, and among the first 35 lawyers to be commissioned in South Carolina.

He was delighted with the prospects in this new country and did all in his power to urge and encourage friends and relatives still in Ireland to come. Two of Parson's nephews, James and O'Brien Smith, were persuaded to emigrate. His lengthy will included them and other family members on condition that they too emigrate. To O'Brien Smith, brother of Honora Smith, James Parsons left much land and property (3). O'Brien, in turn, tried to persuade his brother-in-law, John Pyne to leave Ireland and come to America.

By early 1805 there must have been serious thoughts in the Pyne household in this direction, for we note that just the month before (Dec 1804), John Pyne mortgaged a house and offices in Nenagh to O'Brien Smith (4). That, however, must have been a bad year for the family to consider trans-atlantic travel, what with the death of his only remaining brother, Richard Markham Pyne, and his teenage son John (5), as well a new baby (O'Brien), and his wife's new pregnancy (with Martha). So we must conclude that the trip to America was postponed.

In February 1807 they mortgaged the house and lands to bankers for £1,000 (6). John Pyne must have made final arrangements during that year to settle up his affairs in Ireland, for we find that he arrived in Charleston, South Carolina on 28 February 1808 with his wife and family of five daughters and two sons, almost certainly having left from the port of Cork.

John Pyne bought up land in a part of Colleton County, then known as St. Bartholomew's Parish, as well as in the city, with the help of his brother-in-law, O'Brien Smith (1756-1811). O'Brien Smith had become an American citizen on 1 July 1784 and was the 2nd President of The Hibernian Society. John Pyne became a well to do rice planter. In his will O'Brien Smith left all of his property to John Pyne. These Plantations were "Youghhall", "Litchfield", and "Dunharrow", among others. John Pyne was styled "The Honorable", and is listed in the South Carolina records as "Gentleman" (meaning that he too had entitlement to bear Arms). He thought of himself as "Planter".

In 1790, at the time of the first United States Census, South Carolina functioned as seven Districts, rather than as Counties. While some "counties" did exist then, the Census ignored them. Others did not function in the capacity of County. In some of the Districts (particularly Charleston and Georgetown) the even older Parish bounds, rather than the newer county boundaries, were used as subdivisions.

St. Bartholomews was one of these Charleston District Parishes, that later became Colleton County. By the time of the 1810 Census, Colleton County included the present County bounds, plus what is now the Dorchester County bounds, as well as parts of Charleston County. Earlier, these bounds had, in addition to St. Bartholomew's Parish, included all or parts of St. Paul's Parish and St. George's Dorchester Parish.

This confusion of territory and the propensity of the local Census takers to adhere to old habits of location and naming, resulted in John Pyne's family being counted, but not in Colleton County. His listing for the 1810 Census is found in Charleston County, is mis-spelled as "Pine", and is tabulated under the heading for "O'Brien Smith" (7). He, his wife, the five girls, and the two boys under 10 are readily identifiable. However, another male, 16, who is listed is confusing. Perhaps he was an indentured servant, a related miscounted family member or merely a miscounted visitor. Possibly he belonged not to the John Pyne household, but to the O'Brien Smith household, and thus should have been marked in a different row.

He applied on 3 March 1810 for Citizenship, was admitted denizen on 3 April 1811 and to full citizen two years later on 20 April 1813 (8). He died on 7 June 1813 and is buried in St. Michael's churchyard in Charleston.

Honora Pyne continued on in Charleston for a few years in their house on Church Street, which she sold on 30 Mar 1821 for $12,000 to Catherine Brown (9), removing then to New York City. She died in Newport, Rhode Island on 21 August 1835 (10). Her will was proved in New York on 23 September 1835 (11). John Pyne and Honora Smith Pyne had issue, all of them born in Ireland, as follows:

2	i. John PYNE	b. c. 1790 dsp 1805
3	ii. Isabella PYNE	b. c. 1792 d. 1827 unm
+4	iii. Mary PYNE	b. c. 1793 d. 1861
+5	iv. Margaret PYNE	b. c. 1796 d. 1867
+6	v. Ann Smith PYNE	b. c. 1799 d. 1856
+7	vi. Smith PYNE	b. 1803 d. 1875
8	vii. O'Brien PYNE	b. c. 1805 dsp 1818
+9	viii. Martha PYNE	b. 1806 d. 1852

(1) Apprentice Enrollment Book
(2) Memorials of the Pyne Family, 1919
(3) Probate of South Carolina Wills
(4) The Irish Genealogist, Part IV, 1987
(5) Ennis Chronicle, 3 Oct 1805
(6) Memorials of the Pyne Family, 1919
(7) 1810 Federal Census, Charleston, SC
(8) South Carolina Naturalizations
(9) Mesne Conveyance Office, Charleston; Deed Record Book G9, page 373
(10) Charleston Gazette
(11) Surrogate Court

CHAPTER VI

THE NEW CITIZENS
THE SECOND GENERATION

"I had a dream which was not all a dream"
Lord Byron

+ 4 Mary PYNE^2, second daughter, third child of John and Honora Pyne was born in Ireland c. 1793 and immigrated with her parents to Charleston, South Carolina. There the young woman was married, (lst) on 6 January 1810 by The Rev Mr. Simons to Thomas Holland HUTCHINSON (1). He died at St. Bartholomew's Parish, South Carolina on 17 May 1813, aged 28 (2). They had issue:

+ 10 i. Thomas HUTCHINSON^3, b. c. 1811 in Charleston, SC.

+ 11 ii. Elizabeth HUTCHINSON^3, b. c. 1812 in Charleston, SC; d. after 1885.

She married (2nd) on 29 Dec 1818 at Charleston, SC Charles Dudley MARCH, son of Dr. Clement March and Lucy Dudley Wainwright of Greenland, NH (3). Charles March and Mary Pyne March removed to New York in 1820. She died on 1 Jan 1861 in New York. He died on 3 Dec 1855 in New York. Mary Pyne March and Charles Dudley March had a son:

+ 12 i. John Pyne MARCH^3, b. c. 1819, Charleston, SC; d. 52 Nov 1873

These Hutchinson and March families are more fully discussed in Chapter VII.

+ 5   Margaret PYNE^2, the fourth child of John and Honora Pyne was born in Ireland c. 1796. Coming with them to Charleston in 1808, she married Henry CARY on 21 May 1814 in Charleston. Henry Cary and Margaret Pyne Cary removed to New York about 1820, probably with the March family. She died in 1867 in New York . He died in New York. They had issue as follows:

+ 13   i. Henry CARY^3, b. 1819 d. 1885

This family is more fully discussed in Chapter VIII.

+ 6   Ann Smith PYNE^2, the fifth child of John and Honora Pyne was born in Ireland in 1799. She arrived with the rest of the family in Charleston in 1808. After her father died in 1813, young Ann continued to live with her mother in Mrs. Pyne's house on the west side of Church Street, north of the Baptist Church, between Tradd and Water Streets in the city. It was in this house that she was married on the evening of 25 June 1817 by The Rev Mr. Muhler to Col. James BANKHEAD, son of James Bankhead, Jr. and Christian Miller (4).

James Bankhead was born in Virginia in 1783. He entered the U.S. Army as a Captain of Infantry on 18 Jun 1808. He served with distinction in the War of 1812 and in the Indian Campaigns in Florida, from which he was breveted to Colonel. During the Mexican War, he was breveted again to Brigader General on 29 Mar 1847, because of his gallant actions in the siege of Vera Cruz. He continued in the service until his death in Baltimore, Maryland on 11 Nov 1856.

James Bankhead and Ann Pyne Bankhead had issue as follows:

+ 14   i. James Monroe BANKHEAD[3], b. 1818 d. 1855 unm.

+ 15 ii. Honora Smith BANKHEAD[3], b. 1820 d. 1856

+ 16 iii. John Pyne BANKHEAD[3], b. 1821 d. 1867 unm.

+ 17 iv. Smith Pyne BANKHEAD[3], b. 1823 d. 1868

+ 18   v. Elizabeth Isabella BANKHEAD[3], b. 1826 dsp c. 1885

+ 19 vi. Henry Cary BANKHEAD[3], b. 1828   dsp 1894

This Bankhead family is more fully disussed in Chapter IX.

+ 7   Smith PYNE[2], second son, sixth child, an the only surviving son of John and Honora Pyne was born in Bloomfield Lodge, Nenagh, County Tipperary, Ireland on 9 January 1803. At the age of 5 he came with his parents, five sisters, and younger brother to Charleston, South Carolina. Although his father had died in 1813, this boy's potential was recognized and he was sent off to Eton College, across the Thames River from Windsor, in England in 1817 (5).

H.C. Maxwell Lyte, in his book "A History of Eton College" (6) describes life at that school during the period of Smith's attendance. Parts of that work are worth paraphrasing, to give the reader a view of the rigors of the educational system as well as an understanding of Smith Pyne's upbringing. It is apparent from the Eton School Lists that Smith was enrolled there between about early September 1817 (Michaelmas Term) until early May 1820 (Trinity Term). "Election" took place in the summer, generally near the end of July each year, and we know he arrived "after election" 1817 and left "before election" 1820. So he can be rather closely placed attending school as noted. Dr. John Keate was the Head-Master at Eton during the period of Smith Pyne's attendance.

Mondays, Wednesdays, and Fridays were strict "working days" when the boys had school hours for much of the day. Tuesdays, Thursdays, and Saturdays were "easy" working days when class would not be conducted for the full day. Generally, students were up by six in the morning and at class by nine.

40

The Collegers dined at twelve o'clock every day and supped at six. They assembled in the hall at seven every evening for reading under the care of the captain of the school. At eight the boys recited prayers and were then locked up for the night. Chapel was held at eleven in the morning and at three in the afternoon every day. Boys in the upper forms had to attend class seventeen times during the week; ten for construing and seven for repetition.

Much of the study was Latin and Greek. They read and translated Homer, Lucian, Virgil, and Horace. They read Greek plays, Roman and Greek History. Much writing was required in all languages studied. Grammar, Geography, Literature, Old and New Testament studies, and Algebra were all intensely and deeply examined, memorized, written upon, and discussed. The boys were all expected to be "gentlemen", and the college could add any other subject matter to the study schedule that was deemed "necessary towards making a compleat scholar".

Following completion of his studies, he returned on the ship "Amity" (George Maxwell, Master), before 30 June 1820 to New York (7). The young man had a good, solid, rigorous, formal educational foundation. Upon his return to America, he matriculated at Columbia, from which he graduated in 1823 with a B.A. Degree. He went on to pursue a Master's Degree in Theology, was ordained a Deacon by Bishop Hobart of New York in 1826, and completed his Master's from Columbia in 1827, being also Priested in that year.

Immediately after his Ordination in 1826, (Fig 6) the young Deacon served as Rector to the Parish of St. John's in Elizabeth, NJ, until 1828, when he received a call to Christ Church, Middletown, CT. He served there until 1839, when he became Rector of St. John's, Yonkers, NY, 1839-1841, Rector of Calvary Church, NY, 1841-1844, assistant Minister, St. John's, Washington, DC in 1844, and Rector thereof from 1845-1864.

He had a most distinguished career, being an earnest and sought after preacher. He was granted the Honorary degree of Doctor of Divinity by Hobart College in 1848. He was Rector of "The Church of the Presidents" as St. John's is sometimes called, (Fig 7) and in that capacity counseled, supported, and ministered to all the Presidents of the United States of America from John Tyler to Abraham Lincoln.

Fig 6 Smith Pyne, 1827

He m. Emma Frances Rogers b. 21 Mar 1804, daughter of Henry Rogers and Frances Moore on 23 May 1825 in New York, NY. He died 7 December 1875 in New York and is buried in the Rogers vault in Trinity Church, New York City. She died 11 Jun 1891.

Fig 7 The Rev Smith Pyne, D.D., 1858.

Smith Pyne and Emma Rogers Pyne had issue as follows:

 20   i. John PYNE³   b. 1827 dsp 1827
 21 ii. Susan Augusta PYNE³ b. 1828 dsp 1828
+22 iii. John PYNE³   b. 1830 d. 1881
+23 iv. Henry Rogers PYNE³   b. 1834 d. 1892
 24   v. Susan Augusta PYNE³ b. 1836 d. 1917 unm
+25 vi. Charles March PYNE³ b. 1839 d. 1892
 26 vii. Margaret PYNE³   b. 1841 dsp 1847

8   O'Brien PYNE², the seventh child, and youngest son of
John and Honora Pyne, was born in Ireland c. 1805 and came
with the rest of the family to Charleston in 1808. He is listed in
a deed of 13 Mar 1816 with the other siblings as an heir of his
father (8), but must have dsp about 1818, since he is not shown
in the schedule of the 1820 Census (9).

+9   Martha PYNE², the youngest child of John and Honora
Pyne, was born in Ireland on 28 February 1806. She was a two
year old infant when the family arrived in Charleston, South
Carolina exactly two years later. A few years after her father
died in 1813, she and her sisters Margaret Pyne Cary and Mary
Pyne March and other family members removed to New York
City in 1820. There she made then acquaintance of Gerard
Walton MORRIS, son of Richard Valentine Morris and Anne
Walton, and grandson of Signer of the Declaration of
Independence Lewis Morris of New York. They were married
at the Morris family ancestral Hudson River home of
Morrisania on 8 Oct 1827.

She died on 8 Jun 1852. He died on 15 Jul 1865. Gerard Walton Morris and Martha Pyne had issue as follows:

+27   i. Isabella Pyne MORRIS b. 1828 d. 1850 unm.

+28   ii. Anne Walton MORRIS .b. 1829 d. 1850 unm.

+29 iii. Honora Pyne MORRIS   b. 1831 d. 1866

+30   iv. Gerard Walton MORRIS b. 1833 d. 1875 unm.

+31   v. Mary Pyne MORRIS   b. 1835 d. 1857

+32   vi. John Pyne MORRIS   b. 1837 d. 1868 unm.

+33 vii. Richard MORRIS   b. 1838 d. 1850 unm.

+34 viii. Henry MORRIS   b. 1839 d. 1876 unm.

+35   ix. Arthur Rutherford MORRIS b. 1846 d. 1917 unm.

This Morris family is more fully discussed in Chapter XIII.

CHART of the DESCENDANTS of MARTHA PYNE

	27	Isabella Pyne Morris
	28	Anne Walton Morris
	29	Honora Pyne Morris
	30	Gerard Walton Morris
9 Martha Pyne	31	Mary Pyne Morris
	32	John Pyne Morris
	33	Richard Morris
	34	Henry Morris
	35	Arthur Rutherford Morris

(1) Gazette, SC Historical and Genealogical Magazine, vol xxxiv, p45
(2) Ibid, p96
(3) SC Marriage Settlements, Vol.7, p334-337
(4) Gazette, Ibid, vol xliii, p156
(5) Eton School Lists
(6) Lyte, "A History of Eton College", 1875
(7) Ship Records into New York; 1819-1820
(8) Mesne Conveyance Office, Charleston; Deed Record Book O8, page 102
(9) US Census, South Carolina, 1820

NOTES

47

CHAPTER VII

THE HUTCHINSON and MARCH FAMILIES

"Of loyal nature and of noble mind"
Alfred, Lord Tennyson

+ 4 Mary Pyne[2] (John Pyne[1]) married Thomas Holland HUTCHINSON, who was born c. 1785. This marriage took place in Charleston, SC, on 6 Jan 1810. Although she and her family had recently come from Ireland (in 1808), they had relatives on her mother's side who had resided in South Carolina for some years.

The young couple quickly adapted to the"Plantation" mode of life, living partly in the city and partly in the country. It was while in the latter that young Thomas died at his father-in-law's Plantation in St. Bartholomew's Parish (in what is now a part of Colleton County) on 17 May 1813, only 28 years of age. They had two children:

10   Thomas HUTCHINSON[3]   b. c. 1811 in Charleston, SC.

11   Elizabeth HUTCHINSON[3] b. c. 1812 in Charleston, SC, d. after 1885. She m.(1st) Dr. Alexander Eddy Hosack b. 6 Apr 1805 in NYC, d. 6 Mar 1871 in NYC. No issue. She m. (2nd) Oldofredi di Tudini. No issue.

4   The widow, Mary Pyne Hutchison, and her young children most probably lived with Mary's mother, Honora Smith Pyne in the town house in the City of Charleston. Honora was one of the signatories to a marriage settlement that took place between her daughter and Charles March, five years into her widowhood.

Charles Dudley MARCH was born in 1781 at Greenland, NH. He was the son of Dr. Clement March and Lucy Dudley Wainwright. This family was descended from Hugh March and Judith Knight of Newburyport, MA (1). He married the widow of Thomas Hutchinson, Mary Pyne Huctchinson, in Charleston, SC on 29 Dec 1818 (2). They removed to New York about 1821. He died 3 Dec 1855 in New York, NY and is buried in the March Family Cemetery at Greenland, NH. They had issue as follows:

12   John Pyne MARCH[3] who was born c. 1819 in Charleston, SC. He married Mary L. Lowndes, daugter of Major Rawlins Lowndes, on 31 Jan 1855. She died at New York c. 1880. He died 25 Nov 1873 at New York, NY, and is buried in the old family Cemetery plot in Greenland, Rockingham County, NH. They had issue:

36 i. Charles MARCH[4] b. 23 Sep 1856 in New York.

37 ii. Clement MARCH[4] b. 21 Nov 1862 in New York, NY, d. 23 Mar 1937 in Kinderhook, NY.

CHART of the DESCENDANTS of MARY PYNE

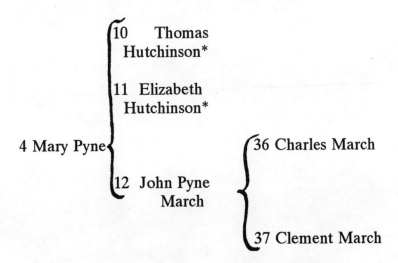

* By first husband Thomas Holland Hutchinson

(1) "The March Family" W. D. Mountain; v3, 1991
(2) SC Marriage Settlements, vol. 7, p 334-337

CHAPTER VIII

THE CARY FAMILY

"What I aspired to be,
And was not, comforts me."
                    Robert Browning

5   Margaret PYNE[2], the third daughter of John Honora Pyne,was courted by a member of an old English and New England family. Henry CARY was most probably born in New England about 1786. He married Margaret Pyne in Charleston, SC on 21 May 1814. They removed to New York about 1820. They had issue:

13 i. Henry CARY[3] who was b. 1819 in Charleston, SC and
    d. 1885 in New York.

CHART of the DESCENDANTS of MARGARET PYNE

5 Margaret Pyne   {13   Henry Cary

CHART of the DESCENDANTS of JOHN PYNE

1 John Pyne

- 2 John Pyne
- 3 Isabella Pyne
- 4 Mary Pyne
  - 10 Thomas Hutchinson
  - 11 Elizabeth Hutchinson
  - 12 John Pyne March
- 5 Margaret Pyne
  - 13 Henry Cary
- 6 Ann Smith
  - 14 James Monroe Bankhead
  - 15 Honora Smith Bankhead
  - 16 John Pyne Bankhead
  - 17 Smith Pyne Bankhead
  - 18 Elizabeth Bankhead
  - 19 Henry Cary Bankhead
- 7 Smith Pyne
  - 20 John Pyne
  - 21 Susan Augusta Pyne
  - 22 John Pyne
  - 23 Henry Rogers Pyne
  - 24 Susan Augusta Pyne
  - 25 Charles March Pyne
  - 26 Margaret Pyne
- 8 O'Brien Pyne
- 9 Martha Pyne
  - 27 Isabella Pyne Morris
  - 28 Anne Walton Morris
  - 29 Honora Smith Morris
  - 30 Gerard Walton Morris
  - 31 Mary Pyne Morris
  - 32 John Pyne Morris
  - 33 Richard Valentine Morris
  - 34 Henry Walton Morris
  - 35 Arthur Rutherford Morris

CHAPTER IX

THE BANKHEAD FAMILY

"...the intrepid and unselfish warrior,
the magistrate who knew no glory
but his country's good"
                    Edward Everett

6   Ann   Smith   Pyne[2] (Fig 9) was   courted by James
Bankhead. Brigader General James BANKHEAD (Fig 8) was
the son of James Bankhead, Jr. and Christain Miller. He was
born in Virginia in 1783. He was commissioned as a Captain of
Infantry 18 Jun 1808. His duties as an Army Officer took him
to Charleston, SC. There he met and married the fourth
daughter of John Pyne, Ann Smith Pyne in her mother's home
on Church Street on 25 Jun 1817. He died in Baltimore, MD
on 11 Nov 1856. She died in Baltimore, MD on 7 Feb 1856.
They had issue as follows:

14   James Monroe BANKHEAD[3] who was born in
        1818 at Charleston, SC. He was a LT in the USN
        and died on duty in Baltimore, MD in 1855, unm.

+15   Honora Smith BANKHEAD[3], b. 17 Feb 1820 in
        Charleston, SC.

Fig 8   BG James Bankhead

Fig 9 Ann Smith Pyne

16   John Pyne BANKHEAD[3] who was born at Fort
      Johnston, Charleston, SC on 3 Aug 1821, became
      a naval Midshipman on 10 Aug 1838. He was
      Commander of the USS Pembina at the Battle of
      Port Royal, SC on 7 Nov 1861, and later was the
      Commander of the US ironclad "Monitor" when
      she foundered off Cape Hatteras on 31 Dec 1862.
      He was later promoted to Captain, US Navy, and
      died on shipboard on his way home from the
      Indian Ocean on 27 Apr 1867 and was buried at
      Aden, Arabia. unm.

+ 17 Smith Pyne BANKHEAD[3], b. 28 Aug 1823 at Fort
      Moultrie, SC

18   Elizabeth Isabella BANKHEAD[3], b. c. 1826 at
      Annapolis, MD, married (1st) Captain William
      H. Ball, USN, on 11 Nov 1857 at Baltimore, MD.
      No issue. He d. 13 Sep 1861. She m. (2nd)
      Francis J. Barretto, who is not the same Francis
      J. Barretto who married Honora Smith Morris in
      1876 (see Chapter XIII). She d. in NYC in Jan
      1894, no issue.

+ 19 Henry Cary BANKHEAD[3], b. 5 Oct 1828 at US
      Arsenal, Pikesville, MD.

15   Honora Smith BANKHEAD[3] (Fig 10), (Ann Smith Pyne[2], John Pyne[1]) b. 17 Feb 1820 in Charleston, SC. She m. 16 May 1848 in Baltimore, MD., George GUEST, the son of John Guest and Rebecca Hall. He was b. in London, ENGLAND on 22 Oct 1806. She d. 18 Apr 1856 at Baltimore, MD. He d. Jul 1879 in Baltimore, MD. They had issue:

+ 38 i.   George   GUEST,   Jr[4],   b.   21   Jun   1851   at Baltimore, MD.

   39 ii. James Bankhead GUEST[4], b. 1853 at Baltimore, MD. He was a member of the New York Stock Exchange and d. 1890, unm.

17   Smith Pyne BANKHEAD[3] (Ann Smith Pyne[2] John Pyne[1]) who was born in 1823 at Fort Moultrie, SC. He took his education at the University of Virginia in Charlottesville. He went on to become a lawyer by profession, but also served as a Captain of Virginia Volunteers at the time of the Mexican War.

   Unlike his father and his older brother John, as well as his younger brother Henry, Smith did not support the Union of the United States during the Civil War, but went with the rebels. He became a Brevet Brigader General of the Confederate Army.

Fig 10 Honora Smith Bankhead Guest
w/ her son George Guest, Jr.

He married Adaline Garth, whose home was "Birdwood". He died in Memphis, TN 1868. Although Mrs. J.E. Warren's Report of the Bankhead Family in "Genealogies of Virginia Families" (1) states there were only four children born of this marriage, records in the family indicate that there were six. They had issue as follows:

40   i. Anne BANKHEAD[4] married MAJ Arthur Allyn, USA, no surviving issue.

41   ii. Ada Pyne BANKHEAD[4] d. unm.

42   iii. William Aubrey BANKHEAD[4], dsp

43   iv. James Wood BANKHEAD[4], dsp

44   v. Florence BANKHEAD[4], dsp

45   vi. Celestine BANKHEAD[4], dsp

19   Henry Cary BANKHEAD[3] was born at the US Arsenal, Pikesville, MD on 5 Oct 1828. He matriculated at Hobart College, Geneva, NY, but later won an appointment to the United States Military Academy at West Point, NY which he entered on 1 Jul 1846. He graduated with the Class of 1850, number 35 in a class of 44 (Graduate # 1484).

He was on frontier duty from 1850-1860. During the Civil War he was Captain of the 5th Infantry, Assistant IG to both the 1st and the 5th Army Corps. He was wounded at Dabney's Mill in Feb 1865, received six Brevets, including Brigader General on 1 Apr 1865 for gallant and meritorious services in the battle of Five Forks.

He died on 9 Jan 1894 at Bayonne, NJ and is buried at Baltimore, MD in Greenmount Cemetery (Area Y, Lot 7). He married Amelia Wainwright, daughter of Bishop Wainwright. She died at Fort Wallace, KS on 13 Aug 1857, no issue.

38 i. George GUEST, Jr[4] (Fig 11), (Honora Smith Bankhead[3], Ann Smith Pyne[2], John Pyne[1]), b. 21 Jun 1851 at Baltimore, MD. He married Sarah Margaret Campbell, daughter of Robert Hamilton Campbell and Eliza Ann Lytle on 22 Apr 1874 in Philadelphia, PA (1). She was b. 8 Sep 1855 in Philadelphia, PA. He died 31 Jan 1881. She m. (2nd) Josiah Low Blackwell, she d. 31 Jan 1890. George Guest and Sarah had three daughters:

59   i. Lily Lytle GUEST[5], b. 15 Feb 1875 in Baltimore, MD. dsp 25 Mar 1899 in Phoenix, AZ.

+ 60 ii. Honora Bankhead GUEST[5], b. 22 Nov 1876 in Baltimore, MD

+ 61 iii. Margaret Biddle GUEST[5], b. 12 Mar 1879 in Baltimore, MD

Fig 11   George   Guest, Jr.

CHART of the DESCENDANTS of ANN SMITH PYNE

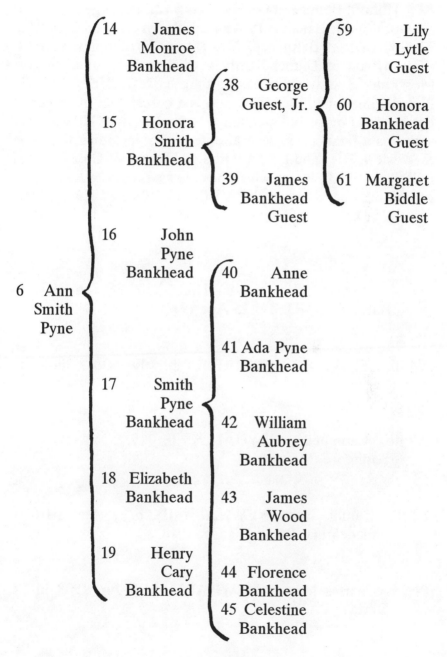

6   Ann
Smith
Pyne

14   James
Monroe
Bankhead

15   Honora
Smith
Bankhead

38   George
Guest, Jr.

39   James
Bankhead
Guest

59   Lily
Lytle
Guest

60   Honora
Bankhead
Guest

61   Margaret
Biddle
Guest

16   John
Pyne
Bankhead

17   Smith
Pyne
Bankhead

18   Elizabeth
Bankhead

19   Henry
Cary
Bankhead

40   Anne
Bankhead

41 Ada Pyne
Bankhead

42   William
Aubrey
Bankhead

43   James
Wood
Bankhead

44   Florence
Bankhead

45 Celestine
Bankhead

65

60   Honora Bankhead GUEST[5] (Fig 12), (George Guest, Jr[4] (Honora Smith Bankhead[3], Ann Smith Pyne[2], John Pyne[1]), b. 22 Nov 1876 at Baltimore, MD (2) m. Thomas NEWHALL (Fig 13) son of Daniel Smith Newhall and Eleanor Mercer Moss on 28 May 1898 in Baltimore, MD. He was b. in Philadelphia on 17 Oct 1876, and is a descendant of Signer of the Declaration of Independence Robert Morris. He was very active as a financier in several enterprises, including the Phila & Western RR, The Penna RR, J.P. Morgan & Co. He was a LCDR in WWI, during which he was awarded the Navy cross for mining operations in the North Sea. He died 9 May 1947. She d. 26 Dec 1946. Thomas Newhall and Honora had five sons (3) (Fig 14):

77   i. Thomas Allerton NEWHALL[6], b. 28 Jun 1900 in Baltimore, MD. dsp 15 Apr 1913.

+ 78   ii.   Blackwell NEWHALL[6], b. 19 Oct 1901 in Baltimore, MD.

+ 79 iii.   Campbell NEWHALL[6], b. 19 Oct 1901 in Baltimore, MD.

80 iv.   Daniel Smith NEWHALL II[6], b. 7 Apr 1903 in Philadelphia, PA; dsp 8 Oct 1918.

+ 81   v. Charles Mercer NEWHALL[6], b. 3 Jun 1908 in St. David's, PA.

Fig 12   Honora   Bankhead   Guest

Fig 13   LCDR   Thomas   Newhall

Fig 14 The Five Newhall sons, 1913
Campbell Newhall Thomas Allerton Newhall Daniel Smith Newhall,II
Blackwell Newhall Charles Mercer Newhall

61   Margaret Biddle GUEST[5], (George Guest, Jr[4] Honora Smith Bankhead[3], Ann Smith Pyne[2], John Pyne[1]), b. 12 Mar 1879 at Baltimore, MD (4), m. Roland Jessup MULFORD (Fig 15) son of Elisha Jessup Mulford and Rachel Price Carmalt in Philadelphia on 21 Dec 1901.

He was a well- known educator, being the Master of St. Mark's School in Southboro, MA; of The Country Day School in Baltimore, MD; of the Cheshire School in CT; and of the Latin School in Princeton, NJ.

He took Holy Orders in the Episcopal Church, being first ordained as Deacon in 1910 and Priested in 1922. He d. in 1951 in Princeton, NJ. She d. in 1962 in Philadelphia, PA. They are both buried in the old family Cemetery plot in Friendsville, PA. Roland Jessup Mulford and Margaret had issue (Fig 16):

+   82   i. Helen Blackwell MULFORD[6], b. 6 Jan 1904 in Cheshire, CT.

+   83 ii. John MULFORD[6], b. 1 Aug 1907 in Cheshire, CT.

78   Blackwell NEWHALL[6], (Honora Bankhead Guest[5], George Guest, Jr[4], Honora Smith Bankhead[3], Ann Smith Pyne[2], John Pyne[1]), b. 19 Oct 1901 in Baltimore, MD; one of a set of twins. He was a graduate of the USNA, class of 1923 (#07004). He m. Mary Large Harrison, daughter of Joseph Harrison and Margaretta Large on 25 Dec 1932 in Bryn Mawr, PA. She was b. 10 Dec 1907 in Colorado Springs, CO. In WWII he was on active duty in the Navy as CDR, during which time he won Commendation from the Secretary of the Navy for bravery in the South Pacific. He returned to business and served as the General Manager of the Board of City Trusts and as a Realtor after his retirement. He d. 20 Oct 1975 in Bryn Mawr, PA and is buried in Old St. David's churchyard, St. David's, PA. They had issue:

96 i. Thomas NEWHALL II[7], one of twins b. 29 Sep 1933 in Philadelphia, PA, dsp 8 Aug 1946 in Centreville, MD.

+ 97 ii. John Harrison NEWHALL[7] (Blackwell Campbell Newhall[6], Honora Bankhead Guest[5], George Guest, Jr[4], Honora Smith Bankhead[3], Ann Smith Pyne[2], John Pyne[1]), b. 29 Sep 1933 in Philadelphia, PA. He took a B.A. from Williams College in 1955 and an M.B.A. from Harvard in 1960. He is a Business Executive. He m. Jane Carol Ward, daughter of Norman S. Ward and Dorothy Williams on 15 Jul 1961 in Maplewood, NJ. They have issue:

Fig 15 Roland Jessup Mulford, c. 1922

Fig 16 Margaret Biddle Guest Mulford w/Children

135   i. Carol Harrison NEWHALL[8], b. 26 Sep 1962 in
      Bryn Mawr, PA. She took a B.A. degree from
      Williams College in 1984. She m. Lewis Levick
      NEILSON, III, son of Lewis Levick Neilson, Jr
      and Caroline Reed Molthan on 29 Jun 1991 at
      Bryn Mawr, PA.

136 ii. Thomas Blackwell NEWHALL[8], b. 6 Sep 1965 in
      Norwalk, CT.

137 iii. Daniel Ward NEWHALL[8], b. 1 Mar 1969 in
      Norwalk, CT.

79   Campbell NEWHALL[6], b. 19 Oct 1901 at Baltimore, MD.
He took a B.A. degree from Harvard in 1924. He worked for
the Baldwin Locomotive Works and travelled a great deal on
their behalf in the west and in Latin America. He m. Margaret
Elizabeth Thomas, daughter of Daniel John Thomas and
Hannah Richards on 15 Mar 1937 in Cleveland, OH. She was
b. on 27 Sep 1904 in Coaldale, PA. He d. in 1963 at Magnolia,
DE; and had issue:

98   i. Honora NEWHALL[7], b. 1 Aug 1939; unm.

74

81   Charles Mercer NEWHALL[6] (Honora Bankhead Guest[5], George Guest, Jr[4], Honora Smith Bankhead[3], Ann Smith Pyne[2], John Pyne[1]), b. 3 Jun 1908 at St. David's, PA. He took a B.S. Degree from University of Pennsylvania in 1931 and became a banker and farmer. He m. Priscilla Jenks, daughter of William Pearson Jenks and Bertha Johnes Cooke, on 3 Jun 1940 at Morristown, NJ. She was b. 10 Oct 1909 in Morristown, NJ. They had issue:

+   99 i. Jennifer NEWHALL, b. 26 Sep 1942 Bryn Mawr, PA.

+ 100 ii. Sally Biddle NEWHALL, b. 12 Feb 1944 in Bryn Mawr, PA.

+ 101 iii. Daniel Smith NEWHALL, b. 23 Aug 1945 in Washington, D.C.

99 i. Jennifer NEWHALL[7], (Charles Mercer Newhall[6] Honora Bankhead Guest[5], George Guest, Jr[4], Honora Smith Bankhead[3], Ann Smith Pyne[2], John Pyne[1]), b. 26 Sep 1942 at Bryn Mawr, PA. She took a B.A. from the University of Pennsylvania in 1966 and an M.Ed. from NYU in 1969. She is a Field Executive with the Morris Area Girl Scout Council. She m. Robert George SALIBA, son of George Joseph Saliba and Katherine Mussawir, on 16 May 1970 at Radnor, PA. He was b. 28 Jan 1940 in Englewood, NJ. They have two children:

138 i. Lynne Newhall SALIBA[8], b. 11 Apr 1972 in Morristown, NJ and now studying at Connecticut College, New London, CT.

139 ii. George Newhall SALIBA[8], b. 21 Aug 1975 in Morristown, NJ.

100 ii. Sally Biddle NEWHALL[7], (Charles Mercer Newhall[6], Honora Bankhead Guest[5], George Guest, Jr[4], Honora Smith Bankhead[3], Ann Smith Pyne[2], John Pyne[1]), b. 12 Feb 1944 in Bryn Mawr, PA. She attended Smith College and later completed her education, receiving a B.A. Degree from Goddard College, VT in 1971. She m. (1st) Perry LEWIS, son of Francis Albert Lewis and Lalite Pepper on 13 Jun 1964 at Kennett Square, PA. He was b. 26 Jun 1942 in Philadelphia, PA. They were divorced in 1985, and she m. (2nd) Thomas Churley Freestone on 26 Oct 1985. He was b. 10 Mar 1923 in Tisbury, Wiltshire, ENGLAND.

Sally Biddle Newhall and Perry Lewis had two children:

140 i. Sally Tyler LEWIS[8], b. 16 Jul 1965 in   Philadelphia, PA. She took a B.A. degree from the   University of Rhode Island in Kingston in 1989.

141 ii. Elizabeth Story LEWIS[8], b. 6 Mar 1968 in Philadelphia, PA. She is a Graduate of the French Culinary Institute of NYC, 1991.

101 iii. Daniel Smith NEWHALL[7], (Charles Mercer Newhall[6] Honora Bankhead Guest[5], George Guest, Jr[4], Honora Smith Bankhead[3], Ann Smith Pyne[2], John Pyne[1]), b. 23 Aug 1945 in Washington, D.C. He studied Electrical Engineering at the University of Pennsylvania. He m. Penelope Jean Pratt, daughter of Thomas Bernard Pratt, Jr. and Julia Eugenia Cox, on 20 Sep 1975 in Wayne, PA. They have two sons:

142 i.   Thomas Pratt NEWHALL[8], b. 25 Oct 1977 in Rockbridge County, VA.

143 ii.   Jonathan Pratt NEWHALL[8], b. 5 May 1981 in Rockbridge County, VA.

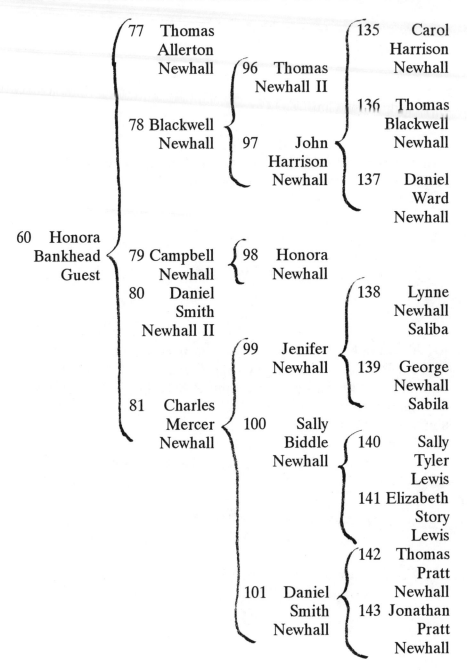

60 Honora Bankhead Guest

77 Thomas Allerton Newhall

78 Blackwell Newhall

96 Thomas Newhall II

97 John Harrison Newhall

135 Carol Harrison Newhall

136 Thomas Blackwell Newhall

137 Daniel Ward Newhall

79 Campbell Newhall

98 Honora Newhall

80 Daniel Smith Newhall II

81 Charles Mercer Newhall

99 Jenifer Newhall

138 Lynne Newhall Saliba

139 George Newhall Sabila

100 Sally Biddle Newhall

140 Sally Tyler Lewis

141 Elizabeth Story Lewis

101 Daniel Smith Newhall

142 Thomas Pratt Newhall

143 Jonathan Pratt Newhall

82   Helen Blackwell MULFORD[6], (Margaret Biddle Guest[5], George Guest, Jr[4] Honora Smith Bankhead[3], Ann Smith Pyne[2], John Pyne[1]), b. 6 Jan 1904 in Cheshire, CT. She m.(1st) Robert Collier WASHBURN, son of Morgan Washburn and Mary Clark on 9 Jun 1927 at Princeton, NJ. They were divorced in 1950. She m. (2nd) Walker Harden; no issue. She d. 10 Apr 1971 at Cambridge, MA. Helen Blackwell Mulford (Fig 17) and Robert Collier Washburn had issue:

+ 102   i. Helen Biddle Guest WASHBURN[7], b. 1 Jul 1928 in NYC.

103 ii. Martin WASHBURN[7], b. 7 Sep 1932 in NYC.

83   John MULFORD[6],(Margaret Biddle Guest[5], George Guest, Jr[4] Honora Smith Bankhead[3], Ann Smith Pyne[2], John Pyne[1]), b. 1 Aug 1907 in Ridgefield, CT. He took a B.A. degree from Princeton in 1929 and a Law Degree from Harvard in 1932. He m. Virginia Compton, daughter of William Compton and Josie McClung. She was b. in 1910 in Waynesboro, VA. He d. in 1984. She d. in 1984. They had issue:

Fig 17 Helen Blackwell Mulford Washburn, 1944

+ 104 i. Joan MULFORD[7], b. 12 Nov 1937 in Philadelphia, PA

105 ii. Jonathan Guest MULFORD[7], b. 7 Apr 1942 in Philadelphia, PA; dsp 1963.

+ 106 iii. Margaret Biddle MULFORD[7], b. 9 Jan 1945 in Philadelphia, PA.

+ 107 iv. Nancy Milton MULFORD[7], b. 12 Nov 1947 in Philadelphia, PA.

102   Helen Biddle Guest WASHBURN[7], (Helen Blackwell MULFORD[6], (Margaret Biddle Guest[5], George Guest, Jr[4] Honora Smith Bankhead[3], Ann Smith Pyne[2], John Pyne[1]), b. 1 Jul 1928 in NYC. She took a B. A. degree from Keuka College, NY in 1950, an M. S. from Simmons Graduate School of Library Science in 1952, and an M.B.A. from Boston University in 1983. She m. Thomas Whipple PERRY, son of Charles Walker Perry and Genevive Estine Pettee on 19 Jun 1951 at Guilford, CT. He was b. 18 Aug 1925. They were divorced on 19 Oct 1985. They had issue:

+ 144   i. Sarah Biddle Guest PERRY[8], (Fig 18) b. 12 Aug 1954 in Elmira, NY.

145 ii. Annah Taft Greene PERRY[8], b. 14 Nov 1955 in Elmira, NY. She took a B.A. from the University of Alaska in 1984, and an M.A. from the University of Wyoming in 1985. unm.

+ 146 iii. Charles Washburn PERRY[8], b. 22 May 1960 in Cambridge, MA.

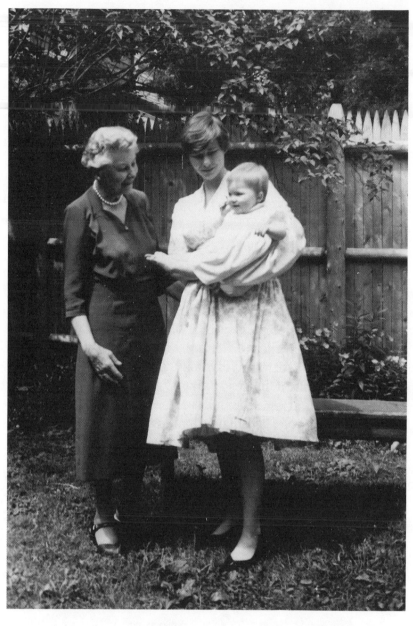

Fig 18 Three Mulford-Biddle Generations, 1955
Margaret Biddle Guest Mulford Helen Biddle Guest Washsburn Perry
Sarah Biddle Guest Perry

104   Joan MULFORD[7], (John MULFORD[6], Margaret Biddle
Guest[5], George Guest, Jr[4] Honora Smith Bankhead[3], Ann Smith
Pyne[2], John Pyne[1]), b. 12 Nov 1937 in Philadelphia, PA. She took a
B.S. degree from the University of Pennslyvania in 1959 and an
M.Ed. from the University of Vermont in 1978. She m. Thedore
Edward BRAUN, Jr., son of Theodore Edward Braun and Mary
Vasche, on 19 Dec 1959 in Bryn Mawr, PA. He was b. on 10 Mar
1934 in Covington, KY. They have issue:

147   i. Theodore Edward BRAUN, III[8], b. 28 Oct 1960 in
       Kansas City, KS. took a B.A. degree from Amherst in
       1982 and a M.F.A. from USC in 1988. umn.

148   ii. Michael Compton BRAUN[8], b. 12 Apr 1963 in
       Philadelphia, PA. He took a B.A. degree from
       Princeton in 1986 and an M.D. from the University of
       Pennslyvania in 1990. He m. Sandra Hurtado De La
       Vega, daughter of Mario Hurtado and Margarita De La
       Vega on 7 Apr 1990 in Jackson, MI. She was b. on 5
       Jun 1963 in New Orleans, LA.

149   iii. Stuart Vasche BRAUN[8], b. 14 Aug 1968 in
       Phildelphia, PA. He took a B.A. from the University of
       Vermont in 1991.

106   Margaret Biddle MULFORD[7], (John MULFORD[6], Margaret Biddle Guest[5], George Guest, Jr[4], Honora Smith Bankhead[3], Ann Smith Pyne[2], John Pyne[1]), b. 9 Jan 1945 in Philadelphia, PA. She took a B.S. degree from the University of Georgia in 1967. She m. (1st) John Calvin HOVER, son of John Curry Hover and Edith Hopkins on 26 Sep 1970 in Bryn Mawr, PA. They were divorced in 1980. She m.(2nd) Edward Kelly Bartholomew on 25 Jun 1988 at Charlotte, VT; no issue. Margaret Biddle Mulford and John Calvin Hover had a child:

> 150 i. Margaret Biddle HOVER[8], b. 5 Dec 1972 in NYC. She is studying at Lehigh University.

107   Nancy Milton MULFORD[7], (John MULFORD[6], Margaret Biddle Guest[5], George Guest, Jr[4], Honora Smith Bankhead[3], Ann Smith Pyne[2], John Pyne[1]), b. 12 Nov 1947 in Philadelphia, PA. She took a B.A. degree from Elmira College in 1969. She m. Douglas Lloyd BURRILL, son of Cecil Burrill and Virginia Parrish on 16 Jun 1979 in Bryn Mawr, PA. He was b. on 16 Aug 1944 in Boston, MA. They have two children:

> 151 i. Cecily Parrish BURRILL[8], b. 14 Dec 1981 in San Francisco, CA.
>
> 152 ii. Julia Lloyd BURRILL[8], b. 16 Aug 1984 in San Francisco, CA.

CHART of MARGARET BIDDLE GUEST DESCENDANTS

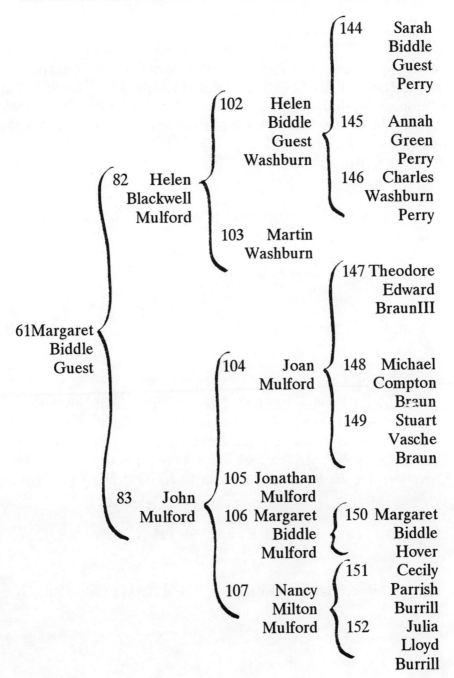

61 Margaret Biddle Guest

82 Helen Blackwell Mulford

102 Helen Biddle Guest Washburn

144 Sarah Biddle Guest Perry

145 Annah Green Perry

146 Charles Washburn Perry

103 Martin Washburn

83 John Mulford

104 Joan Mulford

147 Theodore Edward Braun III

148 Michael Compton Braun

149 Stuart Vasche Braun

105 Jonathan Mulford

106 Margaret Biddle Mulford

150 Margaret Biddle Hover

107 Nancy Milton Mulford

151 Cecily Parrish Burrill

152 Julia Lloyd Burrill

144 Sarah Biddle Guest PERRY[8], (Helen Biddle Guest WASHBURN[7], (Helen Blackwell MULFORD[6], (Margaret Biddle Guest[5], George Guest, Jr[4] Honora Smith Bankhead[3], Ann Smith Pyne[2], John Pyne[1]), b. 12 Aug 1954 in Elmira, NY. She took a B.A. degreee from Franklin & Marshall College in 1976. She m. Charles Lee CORREIA on 31 Dec 1983 at Watertown, MA. They have issue:

173   i. Jonathan Lee CORREIA[9], b. 30 Jan 1985 in Boston, MA.

174   ii. Margaret Guest CORREIA[9], b. 27 May 1987 in Boston, MA.

175   iii. Juliana Taft CORREIA[9], b. 22 Nov 1989 in Cambridge, MA.

146 Charles Washburn PERRY[8], (Helen Biddle Guest WASHBURN[7], (Helen Blackwell MULFORD[6], (Margaret Biddle Guest[5], George Guest, Jr[4] Honora Smith Bankhead[3], Ann Smith Pyne[2], John Pyne[1]), b. 22 May 1960 in Cambridge, MA. He took a B.S. from the Maritime Academy in Galveston, TX. He m. Anita Ranno on 13 Jul 1985. They have issue:

176   i. Evan Thomas PERRY[9], b. 4 Feb 1986 in Galveston, TX.

177 ii. Rebecca Lauren PERRY[9], b. 9 Apr 1989 in Galveston, TX.

CHART of the HELEN BIDDLE GUEST WASHBURN DESCENDANTS

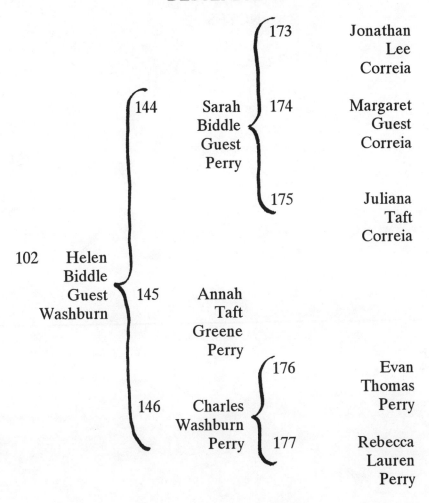

102 Helen Biddle Guest Washburn

144 Sarah Biddle Guest Perry

173 Jonathan Lee Correia

174 Margaret Guest Correia

175 Juliana Taft Correia

145 Annah Taft Greene Perry

146 Charles Washburn Perry

176 Evan Thomas Perry

177 Rebecca Lauren Perry

(1) Genealogies of Virginia Families, v.1 pp 222-232; Wm & Mary Quarterly
(2) Colonial Dames of America, MHS Chart Files, # X-239
(3) Colonial and Revolutionary Families of Pennsylvania; Wilfred Jordan, 1935
(4) Colonial Dames of America, MHS Chart Files, # X-233

NOTES

CHAPTER X

THE PYNE FAMILY as AMERICANS
THE THIRD GENERATION

*"Come Holy Ghost our souls inspire,
And lighten with celestial fire."*
Book of Common Prayer

+ 7 Smith PYNE[2] (John Pyne[1]) was born in Bloomfield Lodge, Nenagh, County Tipperary, Ireland on 9 Jan 1803. He married Emma Frances Rogers, daughter of Henry Rogers and Frances Moore of New York on 23 May 1826. They had issue as follows:

    20 John PYNE[3], b. in Elizabeth, NJ on 3 May 1827, dsp. 4 May 1827.

    21 Susan Augusta PYNE[3], b. in Middletown, CT on Apr 1828 and d. a few hours later the same day.

+ 22 John PYNE[3], b. in Middletown, CT on 16 Oct 1830 (Fig 19).

+ 23 Henry Rogers PYNE[3], b. 3 Jul 1834 in Middletown, CT.

24   Susan Augusta PYNE[3], b. 18 Mar 1836 in Middletown, CT; d. 9 Feb 1907 in New York, NY, unm.

+ 25   Charles March PYNE[3], b. in Jersey City, NJ on 27 Feb 1839.

26   Margaret PYNE[3], b. 29 Jan 1841 in New York, NY, dsp. 2 May 1847 in Washington, DC and is buried in the Congressional Cemetery.

Fig 19 John Pyne, 1860

22   John PYNE[3], third child, eldest surviving son of Smith Pyne, b. in Middletown, CT on 16 Oct 1830. He was educated at St. James College, Hagerstown, MD where he took a Degree in 1848 and an M.A. Degree in 1851. There is an old family tradition that suggests that John Pyne's father presented him with a family crest ring upon his graduation. As an Eton scholar the father would have been aware of the social value of preserving Coat Armour. Such a ring does exist, and has been passed down through John Pyne's great nephew Frederick Glover Pyne to the author. He took the bar examinations and became a Counselor at Law in New York City (Fig 19). He married Anne Cambreleng, daughter of Stephen J. Cambreleng in Apr 1852. He d. 3 Jan 1881. They had no issue.

+ 23   Henry Rogers PYNE[3] (Smith Pyne[2], John Pyne[1]) b. 3 Jul 1834 in Middletown, CT. He also took a B.A. Degree from St. James College in 1853 and an M.A.in 1856. He went on to take Holy Orders and was ordained into the Episcopal Church. He was Chaplain of the 1st New Jersey Cavalry during the Civil War, and author of "The History of the First New Jersey Cavalry", published in 1871. He became Rector of St. Philip's Church, Wiscasset, ME (1877-1889).

He married Elizabeth Ann Frailey, daughter of Dr. Charles C. Leonard Frailey and Caroline Conway of Washington, DC, and d. in that city on 12 Apr 1892. They had issue:

91

+ 46   i. John PYNE⁴, b. 11 Dec 1867 in Holland Patent, Oneida County, NY.

47 ii. Caroline Conway Frailey PYNE⁴ b. 31 Jul 1869 Holland Patent, Oneida County, NY, d. 10 Aug 1944 in Washington, DC, unm.

48 iii. Charles Leonard PYNE⁴, b. 28 May 1871 in Washington, DC, was a Lieutenant in the USNR, and died of injuries while on duty, unm.

49 iv. Henry Rogers PYNE⁴, b. 3 Apr 1873 in Hamilton, NY. He married Ethel Constance Gaertner, daughter of Otto Edward Philip Gaertner and Mary Louise Hageman in Jun 1913. He d. in Washington, DC on 22 Feb 1963 without issue.

46   John PYNE⁴ (Henry Rogers Pyne³, Smith Pyne², John Pyne¹) b. 11 Dec 1867 in Holland Patent, Oneida County, NY. He married (1st) Kathleen Hanrahan of New York on 21 Jul 1890. She d. in NYC. He married (2nd) a wife who d. 1936 at Ward's Island, NY, without issue. John Pyne and Kathleen Hanrahan had issue:

62   i. Katherine PYNE⁵ b. 1892 dsp. 1892

63 ii. Mary PYNE⁵   b. 1893 d. 1919 unm.

64 iii. Helen PYNE⁵   b. 1894 dsp. 1894

+ 65 iv. John PYNE^5 (John Pyne^4, Henry Rogers Pyne^3, Smith Pyne^2, John Pyne^1). This John Pyne was born 10 Feb 1902 in New York. He attended Fordham University. He was an officer in the Naval Reserve and was on active duty during WWII when he d. 25 Mar 1943 in a Jeep accident at West Point, NY.

It is a curious turn of fate that on the occasion of this accident, John's blood second cousin, Frederick Cruger Pyne, was also on active duty with the Army, stationed at West Point as a math Professor, and was the Officer of the Day who first got the notice that there had been an accident near the Post.

John Pyne married Mabel Melvina Mandeville ("Topsy") who was b. 15 Jan 1903, on 2 Mar 1924. She d. Sep 1969; they are both buried at Arlington National Cemetery. They had one child:

+ 84   i. Jennifer PYNE b. 30 Nov 1930 (Fig 20).

Fig 20   Third Cousins, Mar 1943
H.W. Pyne   M.M. Pyne ("Topsy")
M.E. Pyne   Jennifer Pyne

84   Jennifer PYNE[6] (John Pyne[5], John Pyne[4], Henry Rogers Pyne[3], Smith Pyne[2], John Pyne[1]), b. 30 Nov 1930 in New York City. She m. Robert Clyde OLIVER, b. at Newton, MA 17 Nov 1925 on 11 Oct 1952 at the First Congregational Church, Darien, CT. He took a B.S. degree from Brown University in 1947 and an MBA from Boston University in 1950. She has a B.A. from Barnard 1951.

CHART of the DESCENDANTS of HENRY ROGERS PYNE

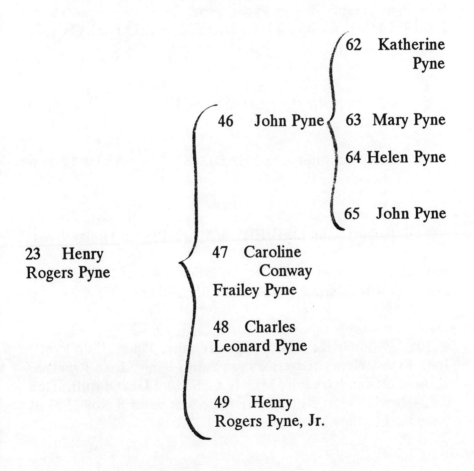

62 Katherine Pyne

46 John Pyne

63 Mary Pyne

64 Helen Pyne

65 John Pyne

23 Henry Rogers Pyne

47 Caroline Conway Frailey Pyne

48 Charles Leonard Pyne

49 Henry Rogers Pyne, Jr.

Robert Clyde Oliver and Jennifer Pyne have issue:

+ 102   i. Sharon Lee OLIVER[7] (Jennifer Pyne[6], John Pyne[5], John Pyne[4], Henry Rogers Pyne[3], Smith Pyne[2] John Pyne[1]) b. 15 Jan 1955 at Ft. Wayne, IN, m. Duane Lee SHADDUCK on 4 May 1974 at Syracuse, NY, and have issue:

> 132   i. Justin Lee SHADDUCK[8], b. 3 Aug 1976 at Edwards AFB, CA
>
> 133 ii. Jennifer Lee SHADDUCK[8], b. 28 Oct 1978 at Edwards AFB, CA

103   ii. Robert John OLIVER[7], b. 3 Apr 1957 at Holland, MI.

104   iii. Susan Ann OLIVER[7], b. 2 Sep 1960 at Holland, MI. She took a B.A. from Ohio University, Athens, OH

+ 105   iv. Peter Kent OLIVER[7] (Jennifer Pyne[6] John Pyne[5], John Pyne[4], Henry Rogers Pyne[3], Smith Pyne[2], John Pyne[1]) b. 22 Aug 1962 in Ferndale, MI. He m. Sandra Deann Buffington on 24 Nov 1989 at Kittery, ME. She was b. on 8 Nov 1963 at Nevada, IA; they have issue:

> 134   i. Matthew Dalton OLIVER[8], b. 8 Jun 1991 at Brighton, MA

CHART of the DESCENDANTS of JOHN PYNE

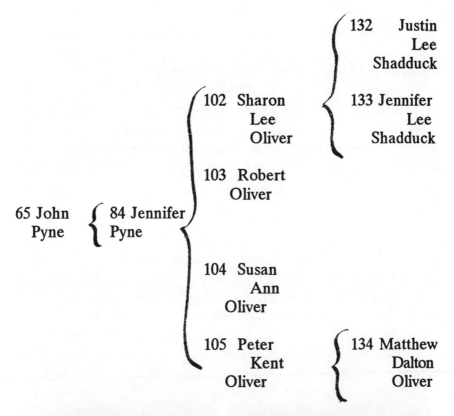

65 John
Pyne
{
84 Jennifer
Pyne

102 Sharon
Lee
Oliver
{
132 Justin
Lee
Shadduck

133 Jennifer
Lee
Shadduck

103 Robert
Oliver

104 Susan
Ann
Oliver

105 Peter
Kent
Oliver
{
134 Matthew
Dalton
Oliver

Fig 21   The Oliver Family, 1990
J.P.Oliver D.L.Shadduck S.O.Shadduck S.B.Oliver P.K.Oliver
Jen.L.Shadduck Jus.L.Shadduck S.A. Oliver R.C.Oliver

97

+23 vi. Charles March PYNE[3] (Smith Pyne[2], John Pyne[1]) youngest son of Smith Pyne and Emma Frances Rogers was born in Jersey City, NJ on 27 Feb 1839. He was educated at St. James College, receiving his B.A. Degree in 1858. On 8 Jul 1858 he became a Corporal in the National Rifles (Company "A"), District of Columbia (Fig 22).

At the very beginning of the Civil War, he volunteered (on 10 Apr 1861), and shortly thereafter was commissioned as 2nd LT, Sixth US Infantry, on 5 Aug 1861 (Fig 23). This unit was with the 5th Corps at the Second Battle of Bull Run, where on 30 Aug 1862, Charles was wounded in the left leg. He was breveted to 1st LT that day "for gallant and meritorious service in the second battle of Bull Run, VA".

Defending his position, even though wounded, his Company was overrun, and he was captured. He was exchanged a few weeks later on 21 Sep 1862. On 8 Aug 1863 he was promoted to 1st LT. The wound failed to respond to several operations and attempts to save it, and the leg finally had to be amputated on 14 May 1864.

Fig 22 CPL Charles March Pyne, 1860
In his uniform of the National Rifles

Fig 23 2nd LT. Charles March Pyne, Aug 1861
As an Officer of the 6th Infantry

He was breveted to Capt on 23 Jan 1865, and promoted to that rank, in the 42nd Infantry, on 28 Jul 1866. From 25 Mar 1867 to 1 Aug 1868 he served as the last Federal Commander of the post at Fort Niagara, NY. He was retired from active military service on 15 Dec 1870, "for disability resulting from wounds received in the line of duty". He was MOLLUS #844.

He then studied at the Berkley Divinity School, Middletown, CT, for Holy Orders and was Ordained a Deacon on 4 Jun 1873, and Priested on 22 Apr 1874. He served in Churches in CT, ME, RI, NJ, and FL. One of the places he served was the very Church of which his father had been Rector, St. John's Church in Washington, DC (Fig 26).

At Middletown, CT he m. Eliza Glover, daughter of Daniel Glover and Ann Mary Cruger on 12 Nov 1873. She was b. in Fairfield, CT on 26 Jun 1847. He died in Elizabeth, NJ on 4 Feb 1892. She d. in Washington, DC on 30 Nov 1920. She is DAR # 3546 and National Society of Colonial Dames of America # 570. Originally buried in Evergreen Cemetary in Elizabeth, NJ, they were both re-interred in Arlington National Cemetery on 13 Apr 1990 (Section 6, 9470 A&B). They had issue:

50   i. Charles Cruger PYNE[4] (Fig 24, 25), b. 29 Sep 1874 in Portland, ME. He was bitten by a rabid dog on 30 Nov 1883, and died in Elizabeth, NJ on 7 Jan 1884. The boy is buried in the Evergreen Cemetery there (Lot 77, Section Q).

*Fig 24 The Rev Charles March Pyne with his wife Eliza Glover
and their young son Charles Cruger Pyne, Jun 1878*

+ 51   ii. John Frederick Glover PYNE[4], b. 5 Jun 1879 (Fig 25, 27), of whom we treat more fully in the next chapter (Chapter XI).

Fig 25 Charles Cruger Pyne and his younger brother Frederick Glover Pyne, Oct 1883

Fig 26 The Rev Charles March Pyne, 1890

52 iii. Francis Rogers PYNE[4], b. 9 Jul 1883 in Elizabeth, NJ. He took a Mining Engineering Degree from Lehigh University, 1906. He married Helen Hastings Johnson, daughter of Theodore Tyler Johnson of Elizabeth, NJ on 28 May 1910.

He was active in his community, serving as a Commisioner for the Boy Scouts of America. He d. 28 Dec 1955 in Elizabeth, NJ. She d. 19 Mar 1963 in Elizabeth, NJ. They are buried in the Evergreen Cemetery there (Lot 77, Section Q). They had twin daughters who died in infancy.

Fig 27 Frederick Glover Pyne, 1895

CHART of the DESCENDANTS of CHARLES MARCH PYNE

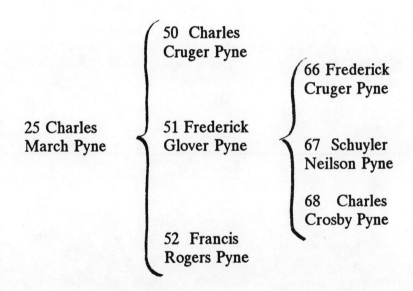

25 Charles
March Pyne

50 Charles
Cruger Pyne

51 Frederick
Glover Pyne

52 Francis
Rogers Pyne

66 Frederick
Cruger Pyne

67 Schuyler
Neilson Pyne

68 Charles
Crosby Pyne

NOTES

CHAPTER   XI

FREDERICK GLOVER PYNE LINE
FOURTH and FIFTH GENERATIONS

"For a man by nothing is so well betrayed as by his manners"
                                                    Edmund Spencer

51 John Frederick Glover PYNE[4] (Charles March Pyne[3], Smith Pyne[2], John Pyne[1]) b. 5 Jun 1879 in Central Falls, RI. As a adult he dropped the "John" and became known as Frederick Glover Pyne. He was educated at Trinity School, following which he became an accountant with the Chemical National Bank in New York.

Fig 28 F.G.Pyne, 1901   *Fig 29 F.G.Pyne, Asst Pay'm*

He wrote and passed the examinations for commission in the US Navy and became Assistant Paymaster on 28 Feb 1901 (Fig 29). He rose through the Supply Corps to the rank of Captain on 29 Nov 1926, retired in 1939 (although he retained a training function) and settled at a place in Cazenovia, NY (purchased in 1930) that he named "Dunharrow" (Fig 30), after one of his great-grandfather's properties in South Carolina. However, he was recalled to active duty in WWII with the retroactive rank of Rear Admiral (Fig 35); and then fully retired on 1 Jul 1944.

Fig 30 "Dunharrow", Summer 1931

He is a descendant, through his mother's line, of GEN Philip Schuyler, was a member of The General Society of Colonial Wars # 6322, Sons of the Revolution # 5046, and MOLLUS #13348.

He married Ellen Roosevelt Jones, daughter of DeWitt Clinton Jones and Josepha Crosby on 23 Sep 1901 in Elizabeth, NJ. She was b. on 23 Feb 1874 in Portland, OR and d. 24 Nov 1954 in Cazenovia, NY. He d. 15 Apr 1962 in Cazenovia, NY. They are buried in Arlington National Cemetery (Section 6, 9470 A&B). They had three sons:

+ 66   i. Frederick Cruger PYNE b. 8 Sep 1902, d. 19 Dec 1984.

+ 67 ii. Schuyler Neilson PYNE b. 24 Sep 1903 d. 13 Jun 1987.

+ 68 iii. Charles Crosby PYNE b. 7 Sep 1905, d. 11 Jun 1962.

Fig 31 CMDR F.G. Pyne & Three Sons, Apr 1925

Fig 32 The Sons, 1908

Fig 33 F.G.P Sons, 1911

Fig 34 Ellen R.Pyne with her Three Sons, 1914
S.N. Pyne   C.C. Pyne   F.C. Pyne

110

Fig 35 Portrait of RADM Frederick Glover Pyne

CHART of the DESCENDANTS of FREDERICK GLOVER PYNE

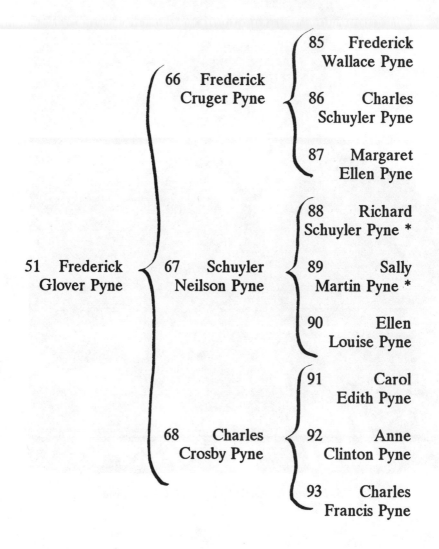

51 Frederick Glover Pyne

66 Frederick Cruger Pyne

85 Frederick Wallace Pyne

86 Charles Schuyler Pyne

87 Margaret Ellen Pyne

67 Schuyler Neilson Pyne

88 Richard Schuyler Pyne *

89 Sally Martin Pyne *

90 Ellen Louise Pyne

68 Charles Crosby Pyne

91 Carol Edith Pyne

92 Anne Clinton Pyne

93 Charles Francis Pyne

* No issue. Each adopted two children.

66 Frederick Cruger PYNE[5] (Frederick Glover Pyne[4], Charles March Pyne[3], Smith Pyne[2] John Pyne[1]), b. 8 Sep 1902 in Agana, Guam, while his father (in the US Navy) was stationed there (Fig 36). He was educated in public and private schools of Elizabeth, NJ and Washington, DC, and won a presidential appointment to the United States Military Academy, which he entered on 1 Jul 1920 (Fig 37), graduating with the class of 1924 (Graduate #7457).

Fig 36 FCP, 1903
with his Mother

Fig 37 Cadet F.C.Pyne, 1921

113

He was a member of Boy Scout Troop 13 in Elizabeth, NJ, and earned the Eagle Rank in 1919. His badge was presented at Madison Square Garden by Lord Baden-Powell on 18 May. During the summers of 1916-1919, he, his brother Schuyler and 4 other scouts from the Elizabeth, NJ Troop, bicycled from there to Cazenovia, NY at which place they created a campsite on the west side of the lake called "Camp Nifty" (Fig 38). The six boys worked for local farmers to earn their money, but also went to the Country Club for dances on the weekends. It was an enlarging and responsible life.

After West Point, young LT Pyne (Fig 39) served in the 82nd Field Artillery Battalion (Horse) at Fort Bliss, TX and at Fort Eustis, VA in the CAC. He resigned from active duty in Nov 1928 and went to work for the Aluminum Company of America, maintaining however, a National Guard or Reserve status (Fig 40). While with Alcoa he lived in Elizabeth, NJ and Pittsburg, PA.(1929-1942).

Fig 38 Camp Nifty, 1919

Fig 39 LT Pyne, 1924   *Fig 40 CAPT Pyne, 1933*

    With the bombing of Pearl Harbor on 7 Dec 1941, he immediately requested return to active duty and was assigned as a Professor of Mathematics at West Point, NY in Jun 1942. He returned to Alcoa in 1945, moving to Michigan. He was Commissioner of Buildings for the little Village of Orchard Lake 1946 -1948, retiring in 1966 to a home in Linwood, MD he had purchased in 1955, against this event.

He married Helen Louise Wallace, daughter of Edward Milne Wallace and Abigail Merriman Noyes on 16 Apr 1925 at St Andrew's Episcopal Church in Washington, DC. She was b. 23 Nov 1903 Lawrence, KS, was a 1924 graduate of Goucher College (B.A.), DAR # 453711 and d. on 18 Feb 1979 in Linwood, MD. He d. on 19 Dec 1984 in Randallstown, MD. They are buried in the Arlington National Cemetery (Section 6, Lot 9468 A). He was DSDI # 1203, SR # 17226, GSCW # 12630, and MOLLUS #19370. They had issue:

+ 85   i. Frederick Wallace PYNE b. 19 Aug 1926

+ 86 ii. Charles Schuyler PYNE b. 17 Sep 1927

+ 87 iii. Margaret Ellen PYNE b.   9 Jun 1929

Fig 41   F.C. Pyne & children, summer 1938
M.E. Pyne F.W. Pyne F.C. Pyne C.S. Pyne

Fig 42   The F. G. Pyne Family, Summer 1949
Back Row: C.C. Pyne   R.S. Pyne   C.S. Pyne   R.W. Patterson   F.W.Pyne
Middle Row: A.C. Pyne   C.E. Pyne   S.M. Pyne   E.B Pyne   M.P. Patterson
Seated: J.M. Pyne F.C. Pyne   E.R. Pyne   F.G. Pyne   H.W. Pyne S.N. Pyne
Ground: E.L. Pyne   Dog Leif   C.F. Pyne

67 Schuyler Neilson PYNE[5] (Frederick Glover Pyne[4], Charles March Pyne[3], Smith Pyne[2] John Pyne[1]) b. 24 Sep 1903 in Elizabeth, NJ. He attended public schools in the area and won an appointment to the United States Naval Academy in Annapolis, MD (Fig 43) from which in graduated in 1925 (#07240). He went on to earn an M.S. degree in Naval Architecture from MIT May 1930.

He was a first class mathematician and Engineer, earning the Order of the British Empire (OBE) and the Legion of Merit (two awards) for his work on construction of vessels and of repair facilities during WW II.

Fig 43 Midshipman S.N. Pyne, 1924

In 36 years of active service with the navy, he rose to the rank of Rear Admiral (Fig 44), retiring in Jun 1961. He continued to work however, first as Deputy Director General of the English Speaking Union, then as a Consultant with EBASCO until 1966 at which time he retired and moved to Annapolis, MD.

118

Fig 44 Portrait of RADM S.N. PYNE

119

He m. Jane Louise Martin (Fig 47) b. 19 Oct 1906, daughter of MG Charles Henry Martin and Louise Jane Hughes on 18 Oct 1930 at Portland, OR. He died 13 Jun 1987 in Annapolis, MD and is buried in the USNA Cemetery. He was a member of the Sons of Revolution #17227, MOLLUS# 20696, the DSDI #1187 of which he was also the

Fig 45 Pyne Men,Aug 1939
C.C. Pyne S.N. Pyne F.C. Pyne F.G. Pyne
R.S. Pyne C.S. Pyne F.W. Pyne

President-General (1964-1967), and an Honorary Member of the Society of the Cincinnati. They had issue:

+ 88   i. Richard Schuyler PYNE b. 26 Jul 1931

+ 89 ii. Sally Martin PYNE b.   17 Apr 1935

+ 90 iii. Ellen Louise PYNE b.   16 Apr 1941

Fig 46 The S.N Pyne Family, 1954
S.M. Pyne S.N. Pyne E.L. Pyne J.M. Pyne R.S. Pyne

120

Fig 47 RADM & Mrs. Schuyler Neilson Pyne, 1960

121

Fig 48 The S. N. Pyne Family, Nov 1970
Standing: R.S. Pyne S.P. Kennedy D.B. Kennedy S.J. Crow
Seated Adults: A.K. Pyne S.N. Pyne J.M. Pyne E.P. Crow
Children: J.F. Pyne M.L.Pyne R.S. Crow K.E. Crow R.W. Crow

68   Charles Crosby PYNE[5] (Frederick Glover Pyne[4], Charles March Pyne[3], Smith Pyne[2] John Pyne[1]), b. 7 Sep 1905 in Pensacola, FL.   He was educated at the Pingry School, Elizabeth, NJ; attended (Fig 49) and Graduated from the US Naval Academy, Class of 1927 (#08692).

Fig 49 C.C. Pyne, 1924   *Fig 50 LCDR Pyne, 1943*

He resigned from active duty in 1929, and worked for the New England Electric System until called up from reserve status in early 1942 (Fig 50). He rose to the rank of Captain, returning to reserve status after WWII.

123

Like both his brothers, Charles was mathematically and scientifically oriented. He was also a socially gifted charmer, and a careful educator of his children. He purchased property at 4 Mansion Road, Marblehead, MA in May 1910. He was Chairman of the Town Finance Committe and Chairman of the Board of the Tower School.

After working for the Joint Research and Development Board at the Pentagon under Vanevar Bush right after the war, he was hired by Harvard University, in 1948, becoming Bursar in 1956 (Fig 51), and holding that position until his death on 11 Jun 1962 in Cambridge, MA. His ashes were scattered in Marblehead Harbor, and a Memorial Window is dedicated to him at St. Andrew's Episcopal Church in Marblehead. He was SR # 17258.

He m. Elisabeth Brown b. 29 Nov 1907 at Winchester, MA on 5 May 1930. She d. 24 Jan 1990 at Norfolk, MA, and her ashes were scattered at St. Andrew's Church, Marblehead, where she is commemorated by a memorial plaque. Charles Crosby Pyne and Elisabeth Brown had issue:

+ 91   i. Carol Edith PYNE   b. 4 Jun 1934

+ 92 ii. Anne Clinton PYNE   b. 25 Feb 1938

+ 93 iii. Charles Francis PYNE b. 29 Jan 1944

Fig 51 Charles Crosby Pyne, 1950

NOTES

126

CHAPTER XII

THE COUSINS, THE SIXTH and SEVENTH GENERATIONS

"...some adventures they had in youth together"
                                        Sir Richard Steele

85   Frederick Wallace PYNE[6](Frederick Cruger Pyne[5], Frederick Glover Pyne[4], Charles March Pyne[3], Smith Pyne[2], John Pyne[1]) b. 19 Aug 1926 at Fort Bliss, El Paso, TX. He was educated in the public schools of NJ, PA, and NY. As soon as he became eligible he volunteered for the service, was in the infantry for 4 years during and after WWII, won a competitive appointment to West Point, which he entered on 1 Jul 1948, and resigned on 15 Oct 1948. He matriculated at Tri-State College in Angola, IN, from which he graduated B.S.C.E on 8 Jun 1951. He took an M.S.E. degree from Johns Hopkins University, Jun 1966. During 40 years he served as an engineer for municipal, state, and federal governments.

He was County Surveyor of Carroll County, MD from 1966-1974. He was a Professional Engineer, was elected a Fellow of the American Society of Civil Engineers (F. ASCE), and was, in retirement, an Adjunct Professor of Mathematics at Frederick Community College.

127

He has been very active as a volunteer with the Boy Scouts of America, serving as a Scoutmaster (1961-1965) in the Town of New Windsor, but mostly as a Commissioner.

At St.James Episcopal Church in Birmingham, MI on 18 Jul 1952 he married Jo Ann Rammes (Fig 52). She was the adopted daughter of Jack Albert Rammes and Irlby Jo Houston of Sylvan Lake, MI. She was the illegitimate daughter of Rosilla Bennett and Robert LaVern Miller b. 8 Jun 1929 in Grand Rapids, MI., named by her birth mother as Donelda Jane Bennett.

She graduated from Oberlin College Jun 1951, B.A. and took an MEd degree from Western Maryland College, Westminster, MD in Jun 1968. She has been quite active as a volunteer with the Frederick County Literacy Council and the AAUW, serving on the Boards of both groups.

Fig 52 F.W. Pyne Wedding, 1952

Like his grandfather, he had purchased a property in the countryside. His was in the village of Linwood, MD located in the western part of Carroll County about halfway between the towns of New Windsor and Union Bridge. This property was purchased in 1954 and was named "Hedgeleigh" (Fig 53). In it the family lived for 32 years. The home is in an Historic District listed in the National Register of Historic Places.

Fig 53 "Hedgeleigh"

He was President-General of the Descendants of the Signers of the Declaration of Independence (1975-1978), #1305, is a member of SAR, #133818, The General Society of Colonial Wars, # 17982, The Sons of the Revolution, # 27234, and The Military Order of the Loyal Legion # 20811. They had issue as follows:

+106 i. Stephen Van Rensselaer PYNE b. Gettysburg, PA 30 Mar 1960

+ 107 ii. Anne Wallace PYNE b. Gettysburg, PA 6 Feb 1962.

+ 108 iii. Elizabeth Glover PYNE b. Gettysburg, PA on 16 Mar 1963.

+ 109 iv. Mary Clinton PYNE b. Gettysburg, PA 19 Oct 1965.

106 Stephen Van Rensselaer PYNE[7] (Frederick Wallace Pyne[6], Frederick Cruger Pyne[5], Frederick Glover Pyne[4] Charles March Pyne[3], Smith Pyne[2] John Pyne[1]) b. Gettysburg, PA 30 Mar 1960 He was educated in the Maryland public schools and at McDonogh School, Ownings Mills, MD (Class of 1979). After some college work at Ohio University and service in the U.S.Navy, he m. (1st) Taya L. Fleming on 11 Aug 1984 in Angola, IN. They were divorced on 3 Mar 1986 in Fort Wayne, IN, no issue.

He took an A.A. degree from Catonsville Community College, 1987 and a B.S. degree from Western Maryland College in May 1988. He has been a member of the Board of the DSDI, is very interested in history and genealogy. He is a member of MOLLUS # 21834, SAR # 134381, SR # 27235, DSDI # 1811, and GSCW # 17983. He is an employee of the Carroll County government and resides near Westminster, MD.

107 Anne Wallace PYNE[7] (Frederick Wallace Pyne[6], Frederick Cruger Pyne[5], Frederick Glover Pyne[4] Charles March Pyne[3], Smith Pyne[2] John Pyne[1]) b. Gettysburg, PA 6 Feb 1962. After attending Catonsville Community College and some service in the U.S. Navy, she m. Jeffrey Ross MARR, b. 26 Jul 1961 in Saginaw, MI at Westminster, MD on 26 Dec 1981. She is DSDI # 1854. They have issue:

135 i. David Benjamin MARR b. 4 Aug 1982 at Cherry Point, NC DSDI # 927 (Jr)

136 ii. Sarah Louise MARR b. 14 Mar 1984 at Cherry Point, NC DSDI # 928 (Jr)

137 iii. Katherine Marie MARR b. 2 May 1988 at Frederick, MD DSDI # 929 (Jr)

108   Elizabeth Glover PYNE[7] (Frederick Wallce Pyne[6], Frederick Cruger Pyne[5], Frederick Glover Pyne[4] Charles March Pyne[3], Smith Pyne[2] John Pyne[1]) b. Gettysburg, PA on 16 Mar 1963. She was educated in the public schools of Maryland and for two years (1977-1979) at the McDonogh School.

She served for 2 years in the US Air Force, m. (1st) William Harold Trainer on 20 Nov 1981 at Minot AFB Chapel, ND. They were divorced on 24 Jan 1983 in Minot, ND no issue. She is DSDI # 1902, and now resides in California.

109 Mary Clinton PYNE[7] (Frederick Wallce Pyne[6], Frederick Cruger Pyne[5], Frederick Glover Pyne[4] Charles March Pyne[3], Smith Pyne[2] John Pyne[1]) b. Gettysburg, PA 19 Oct 1965. She was educated in the Maryland public schools, went to the Catonsville Community College for a year, and transfered to Harding.

She graduated from Harding University, Searcy, AR with a B.A. degree in May 1988, and m. David Kim SMELSER b. 25 Sep 1966 in Seoul, KOREA, in Frederick, MD on 24 Nov 1988. She is a teacher in the Frederick County School System. She is a Life Member of the DSDI, # 1980, and is now pursuing an advanced degree from Hood College, Frederick, MD.

CHART of the DESCENDANTS of FREDERICK WALLACE PYNE

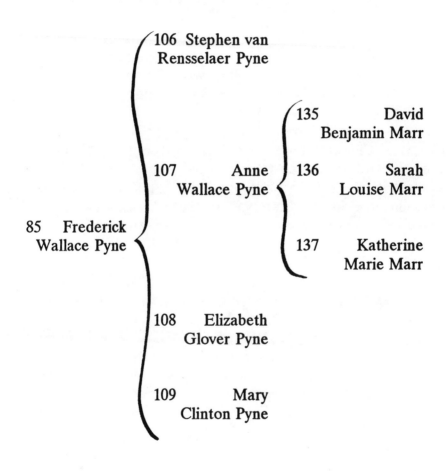

106 Stephen van Rensselaer Pyne

135 David Benjamin Marr

107 Anne Wallace Pyne

136 Sarah Louise Marr

137 Katherine Marie Marr

85 Frederick Wallace Pyne

108 Elizabeth Glover Pyne

109 Mary Clinton Pyne

Fig 54 The F.C. Pyne Family, 1960
C.S. Pyne F.W. Pyne A.R. Pyne w/SVRP R.W. Patterson
V.S. Pyne w/MRP H.W. Pyne F.C. Pyne M.P. Patterson

86   Charles Schuyler PYNE[6] (Frederick Cruger Pyne[5], Frederick Glover Pyne[4] Charles March Pyne[3], Smith Pyne[2], John Pyne[1]) b. 17 Sep 1927 at Fort Bliss, El Paso, TX. He enlisted in the cavalry for 3 years, completing his basic training at Ft. Riley, KS in Dec 1945 in the last Horse Cavalry outfit in the U.S. Army, spent an academic year in the USMA Preparatory School at Stewart Field, NY in 1947-48, took a B.S.Ch.E on 8 Jun 1951 from Tri-State College. He m. Leora Virginia Smith, b. 5 Jun 1925 in York Township, IN, the daughter of Henry Paul Smith and Zema Iona Peet, on 26 Aug 1950 in Angola, IN. She is DAR # 653814.

135

He was an executive with Goodyear International Corporation (GIC). For them he built a chemical plant in Le Havre, France, and also in Rio de Janeiro, Brazil (Fig 55). He had a strong interest in history and fencing, winning many tournament championships. A Memorial Sabre Trophy has been established at Tri-State in his name. The Alumni Distinguished Service Award was presented posthumously in 1976. He was DSDI # 1374. He died in an auto accident in San Paolo, Brazil 29 Nov 1975, and was buried in Circle Hill Cemetery, Angola, IN. Issue (Fig 56):

+ 110 i. Catharine Clarkson PYNE b. 6 Aug 1952 Akron, OH.

+ 111 ii. Philip Schuyler PYNE b. 11 Feb 1956 in Minneapolis, MN.

+ 112 iii. Margaret Rogers PYNE b. 3 Jan 1959 Brussels, BELGIUM.

+ 113 iv. David Wallace PYNE b. 23 Oct 1960 Brussels, BELGIUM.

114 v. Christopher Cruger PYNE b. 18 Jan 1966 in Akron, OH. dsp 4 Dec 1975 in Sao Paulo, BRAZIL.

110 Catharine Clarkson PYNE[7] (Charles Schuyler Pyne[6], Frederick Cruger Pyne[5], Frederick Glover Pyne[4], Charles March Pyne[3], Smith Pyne[2], John Pyne[1]) b. 6 Aug 1952 Akron, OH. She attended Akron University. She was DSDI# 1582. She m. (1st) Joseph C. DiGIACOMO on 17 Jun 1972 in Akron, OH. They were divorced on 5 Jan 1987 in Akron, OH and had issue:

139   i. Catharine Silvia DiGIACOMO b. 10 Aug 1975
Akron, OH

140   ii. Virginia Claudia DiGIACOMO b. 10 Aug 1975
Akron, OH

141 iii. Joseph Christopher DiGIACOMO b. 7 Jul 1978
Akron, OH

She m. (2nd) David Michael Cross on 17 Dec in Akron, OH. He is the son of James Oliver Cross and Josephine Helen Smith b. 24 Oct 1951 Akron, OH. This couple had previously had issue:

138   i. Frederick Michael PYNE b. 28 Feb 1970 Toledo, OH and adopted by others as Kent Alan Waugh

111 Philip Schuyler PYNE[7] (Charles Schuyler Pyne[6], Frederick Cruger Pyne[5], Frederick Glover Pyne[4], Charles March Pyne[3], Smith Pyne[2], John Pyne[1]) b. 11 Feb 1956 in Minneapolis, MN. He was educated in private schools in Brussels and Paris, graduating from the Escola Graduada de Sao Paulo in Brazil. He attended Bowling Green University in Ohio and took a B.S. degree from Ball State University in Muncie, IN May 1981. His business career has centered around the transportation industry in sales and management. He is DSDI # 1742. He m. Ellen Jamieson Hammill at St. Peter's Episcopal Church in Philadelphia, PA on 25 Aug 1990. She is the daughter of James Clarence Hamill and Judith Ellen Dry, b. 1 Jul 1961 in Greer, SC. She took a B.A. in Elementary Education from the University of South Carolina, where she also studied law.

112   Margaret Rogers PYNE[7] (Charles Schuyler Pyne[6], Frederick Crugor Pyne[5], Frederick Glover Pyne[4], Charles March Pyne[3], Smith Pyne[2], John Pyne[1]) b. 3 Jan 1959 in Brussels, BELGIUM. She took a B.A. degree from Ball State University May 1981. She has been very interested in computer teaching programs for children. She m. Scott Simmons LUNDIE on 19 Jun 1982 in Angola, IN. He is the son of Stuart Stevenson Lundie and Ann Drummond Simmons, b. 8 Oct 1959 in Angola, IN. She is DSDI # 1792. They have issue (Fig 57):

142   i. Tara Ellen LUNDIE[8] b. 24 Nov 1986 Carrollton, TX

143 ii. Alexander Simmons LUNDIE[8] b. 15 Feb 1989 in Ridgewood, NJ.

113   David Wallace PYNE[7] (Charles Schuyler Pyne[6], Frederick Cruger Pyne[5], Frederick Glover Pyne[4], Charles March Pyne[3], Smith Pyne[2], John Pyne[1]),b. 23 Oct 1960 in Brussels, BELGIUM. He attended college at Bakersfield, CA, and has been working for the banking industry in Wilmington, DE. He m. Keyla Ines Rivero 20 Jan 1990 in Claymont, DE. She is the daughter of GEN Oswaldo DeJesus Rivero Ochoa and Keyla Ines Rodriquez Ochoa, b. 5 Jun 1962 at Aberdeen Proving Ground, MD. He is DSDI # 1893. They have issue:

144   i. Edward Wallce PYNE[8] b. 8 Aug 1990 in Wilmington, DE.

138

CHART of the DESCENDANTS of CHARLES SCHUYLER PYNE

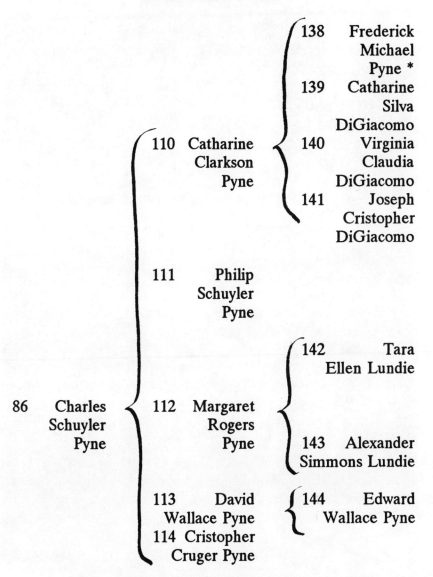

86 Charles Schuyler Pyne

110 Catharine Clarkson Pyne

    138 Frederick Michael Pyne *

    139 Catharine Silva DiGiacomo

    140 Virginia Claudia DiGiacomo

    141 Joseph Cristopher DiGiacomo

111 Philip Schuyler Pyne

112 Margaret Rogers Pyne

    142 Tara Ellen Lundie

    143 Alexander Simmons Lundie

113 David Wallace Pyne

114 Cristopher Cruger Pyne

    144 Edward Wallace Pyne

* Illegitimate child of Catharine Clarkson Pyne and David Michael Cross, adopted as Kent Alan Waugh by others; Cross-Pyne later marrying.

Fig 55 Portrait of Charles Schuyler Pyne, 1975

Fig 56 The C.S. Pyne Family, Aug 1963
C.S. Pyne C.C. Pyne   D.W. Pyne V.S. Pyne
P.S. Pyne   M.R. Pyne

Fig 57   The Lundie Family, 1990
Scott   Alex   Tara   Peggy

87   Margaret Ellen PYNE[6] (Frederick Cruger Pyne[5], Frederick Glover Pyne[4], Charles March Pyne[3], Smith Pyne[2], John Pyne[1]), b. 9 Jun 1929 in Elizabeth, NJ. m. Robert Williams PATTERSON, son of Donald Stanton Patterson and Mary Joyce Hodges, on 21 Aug 1940 in Pontiac, MI at All Saints Episcopal Church (Fig 58). He took a B.A. from Alma College, MI, 1951 and was a law student at University of Michigan. She is DSDI # 1521, and DAR # 455386. They have issue (Fig 59):

+115   i. Margaret Wallace PATTERSON b. 10 Jun 1952
       Ann Arbor, MI.

 116 ii. Robert Clinton PATTERSON b. 9 Jan 1959 at
       Beaumont Hospital, Royal Oak, MI. He was a student
       at University of Vincennes, IN. He works for the State
       of Indiana. He is DSDI # 1805, unm.

115   Margaret Wallace PATTERSON[7] (Margaret Ellen Pyne[6], Frederick Cruger Pyne[5], Frederick Glover Pyne[4], Charles March Pyne[3], Smith Pyne[2], John Pyne[1]) b. 10 Jun 1952 Ann Arbor, MI. She is DSDI # 1580. She took a B.S. degree from Purdue Universty in May 1974. She has been a teacher in various school systems. She m. Thomas Charles WHITELOCK on 5 Apr 1975 at St. Paul's Episcopal Church, Indianapolis, IN. He was b. 27 Jul 1952. He is a graduate of Ferris State University, Big Rapids, MI, and works for a division of General Motors. They have issue:

 145 i. Andrew Charles WHITELOCK[8] b. 2 Nov 1979
       Lafayette, LA. DSDI # 923 (Jr)

 146 ii. James Thomas WHITELOCK[8] b. 29 Jun 1982
       Lafayette, LA. DSDI # 924 (Jr).

Fig 58 Margaret Ellen Pyne Wedding, 1948

143

CHART of the DESCENDANTS of MARGARET ELLEN PYNE

87 Margaret Ellen Pyne

115 Margaret Wallace Patterson

116 Robert Clinton Patterson

145 Andrew Charles Whitelock

146 James Thomas Whitelock

Fig 59 The Patterson Family

Bob   Peggy   Meg   Robbie

144

88   Richard Schuyler PYNE[6] (Schulyer Neilson Pyne[5], Frederick Glover Pyne[4], Charles March Pyne[3], Smith Pyne[2], John Pyne[1]), b. 26 Jul 1931 Philadelphia, PA. He was educated at the South Kent School, CT, the Bullis School, and the US Naval Academy, Class of 1955 (non-graduate). He went on to the Marine Corps, rose to the rank of LTC, retired, moved to Pensacola, FL, and earned a B.S. degree from the University of Western Florida in Dec 1984.

He m. Alice Leith Kepler, daughter of George Alfred Kepler and Sue Gaby Meng, on 12 Aug 1961 at San Diego, CA. She was born 9 Jan 1939 in Port Deposit, MD. She had completed nursing training at Good Samaritan Hospital in Phoenix, AZ in 1959 and served as a Navy Nurse 1960-1962. They adopted two children:

i. Margaret Louise PYNE, b. Honolulu, HI 4 Nov 1964; m. Eric Matthew Scheulin at Pensacola, FL on 4 Nov 1989.

ii. John Frederick PYNE, b. Hickory, NC 16 Sep 1968. He had studied for a B.S. in Criminal Justice at the University of Western Florida, and is now a Highway Patrol Officer for the State of Florida.

89 Sally Martin PYNE[6] (Schulyer Neilson Pyne[5], Frederick Glover Pyne[4], Charles March Pyne[3], Smith Pyne[2], John Pyne[1]), b. 17 Apr 1935 Bremerton, WA. m. David Boyd KENNEDY, son of James Alexander Kennedy and Elizabeth Earhart, b. 2 Sep 1933 in Ann Arbor, MI at Seattle, WA on 31 Oct 1961. She has been very active with the Experiment in International Living (EIL). She is DSDI # 1226. They adopted two children:

      i. Jane Elizabeth KENNEDY b. 22 Jan 1971 Newcastle, WY and is now pursuing a B.A. degree from Washington College, Chestertown, MD.

      ii. Douglas Earhart KENNEDY b. 7 Mar 1973 Larimie, WY. He is now studying at Chesapeake College, Wye Mills, MD.

90 Ellen Louise PYNE[6] (Schulyer Neilson Pyne[5], Frederick Glover Pyne[4], Charles March Pyne[3], Smith Pyne[2], John Pyne[1]) b. 16 Apr 1941 Washington, DC. She is a graduate of the Holton Arms School and Bradford Junior College, MA. She m (1st) Capt. Stuart Joseph CROW, b. 6 Jul 1939, the son of William Hampton Crow and Anita Charlotte Wiedermayer, at Short Hills, NJ on 14 Sep 1963. He was graduated from the Pingry School and took a B.S. degree from Virginia Military Institute. She is DSDI # 1287.

They were divorced on 18 Sep 1985 at Annapolis, MD. She m. (2nd) Erik Freit on 16 Sep 1986. They were divorced in 1988. No issue from this second marriage. She m. (3rd) John Kenneth Toay at Annapolis, MD on 11 Nov 1991.

Ellen Louise Pyne and Stuart Joseph Crow had issue:

117   i. Richard William CROW[7] b. 23 Dec 1964 at Ft. Lewis, WA. He took a B.A. degree from Ripon College, WI in May 1987 and currently works for Federal Express.

118   ii. Robert Schuyler CROW[7] b. 20 Sep 1966 at Annapolis, MD. He took a B.S. Degree in Engineering from Virginia Military Institute in 1988 and was commissioned in the USAF and participated in the Persian Gulf War. He m. Rachael Lee Stouch at Charleston, WV on 10 Sep 1988.

119   iii. Karen Elizabeth CROW[7] b. 30 May 1968 at Annapolis, MD. She took a B.S. degree from the University of New Hampshire in 1990.

120   iv. Catherine Louise CROW[7] b. 20 Nov 1971 in Honolulu, HI.

CHART of the DESCENDANTS of ELLEN LOUISE PYNE

90	Ellen Louise Pyne	117	Richard William Crow
		118	Robert Schuyler Crow
		119	Karen Elizabeth Crow
		120	Catherine Louise Crow

91   Carol Edith PYNE[6] (Charles Crosby Pyne[5], Frederick Glover Pyne[4], Charles March Pyne[3], Smith Pyne[2], John Pyne[1]), b. 4 Jun 1934 in Boston, MA. She took a B.A. from Wellesley College in 1956. She m. Max Rudolph SCHREIBER b. North Hollywood, CA 14 Jun 1931 at Marblehead, MA on 2 Apr 1960. He is the son of Werner Kurt Schreiber b. Berlin, GERMANY, 29 Nov 1903, d. Sep 1952 and Lili Wilhermina Bausch, b. Anspach, Taunus, GERMANY, 31 Jul 1907. They have issue (Fig 60):

121 i. Rolf Gregory SCHREIBER[7] b. Salem, MA on 27 Sep 1961. He graduated from The University of CA, San Diego (UCSD) Jun 1985 and m. at Orinda, CA on 2 May 1987 Lisa Christine Hill, daughter of Hal H. Hill and Diane Frazier, b. at Berkely, CA on 9 Mar 1963. She Graduated from UCSD in Jun 1986.

122 ii. Christina Anne SCHREIBER[7] b. Salem, MA on 30 Jan 1963. She graduated from Wellesley College in May 1985. She is DSDI # 2130.

CHART of the DESCENDANTS of CAROL EDITH PYNE

91   Carol
Edith Pyne

{ 121   Rolf
Schreiber

122   Christina
Schreiber

Fig 60   The Schreiber Children, Aug 1965
Rolf and Christina

92   Anne Clinton PYNE[6] (Charles Crosby Pyne[5], Frederick Glover Pyne[4], Charles March Pyne[3], Smith Pyne[2], John Pyne[1]) b. 25 Feb 1930 in Boston, MA. She took a B.A. from Wellesley in 1959 and a PhD in Astronomy from the University of Michigan in 1963.

She helped to discover the "black hole", and has been teaching and researching in this field. She m. Charles Ramsey COWLEY b. 13 Sep 1934 in Agana, GUAM, on 9 Jun 1960 at Marblehead, MA. They were divorced on 8 Apr 1983 at Ann Arbor, MI. They had issue:

123 i. David Moncure COWLEY[7] b. 18 Apr 1965 in Elkhorn, WI. He Graduated from Arizona State University Dec 1989.

124 ii. James Robert COWLEY[7] b. 13 Jan 1968 in Pontiac, MI

CHART of the DESCENDANTS of ANNE CLINTON PYNE

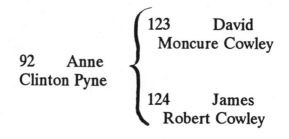

92   Anne Clinton Pyne

123   David Moncure Cowley

124   James Robert Cowley

93 Charles Francis PYNE[6] (Charles Crosby Pyne[5], Frederick Glover Pyne[4], Charles March Pyne[3], Smith Pyne[2], John Pyne[1]) b. 29 Jan 1944 in Boston, MA. He was educated at Governor Dunmore Academy in MA, graduated from Harvard University with a B.A. in Applied Mathematics, Jun 1967. He set up and is CEO of his own consulting company, Pyne Associates. He m. Mary Elizabeth Merrick on 6 Aug 1966 at Marblehead, MA. He is DSDI # 2059. They have issue (Fig 61):

125   i. Charles Crosby PYNE II[7] b 20 Dec 1973 at Norwood, MA.

126 ii. Sarah Elizabeth PYNE[7] b. 5 Apr 1977 at Norwood, MA.

CHART of the DESCENDANTS of CHARLES FRANCIS PYNE

93   Charles Francis Pyne

125   Charles Crosby Pyne II

126   Sarah Elizabeth Pyne

Fig 61 The C.F. Pyne Family, 1990
E.M. Pyne S.E. Pyne C.F. Pyne C.C. Pyne II
151

NOTES

CHAPTER XIII

THE MORRIS FAMILY

*"The truly noble and resolved spirit raises
itself, and becomes more conspicuous in times
of disaster and ill fortune"*

Plutarch

9   Martha Pyne[2] was courted by Gerard Walton MORRIS
who was the 2nd child, 2nd son of Richard Valentine Morris,
who was the youngest(10th) child of Lewis Morris, one of the
four New York Signers of the Declaration of Independence (1).

Gerard Walton Morris was born in New York, NY 11
Jul 1799. He married Martha Pyne, youngest daughter of John
Pyne and Honora Smith Pyne in Morrisania, Westchester
County, NY on 8 Oct 1827. They had nine children, of whom
only two married and had issue. He died in New York City on
19 Jul 1865. She died in Morristown, NJ on 8 Jun 1852. The
children of Gerard Walton Morris and Martha Pyne Morris
were:

27   i. Isabella Pyne MORRIS[3], b. New York, NY 28 Jul 1828 d. New York, NY 28 Aug 1851 unm.

28 ii. Anne Walton MORRIS[3], b. New York, NY 13 Dec 1829 d. New York, NY 22 Feb 1850 unm.

+ 29 iii. Honora Smith MORRIS[3], b. New York, NY 2 Sep 1831.

30 iv. Gerard Walton MORRIS[3], b. New York, NY 30 Dec 1833 d. France 10 Oct 1875 unm.

+ 31   v. Mary Pyne MORRIS[3], b. New York, NY 3 May 1835

32 vi. John Pyne MORRIS[3], b. New York, NY 13 Jan 1837 d. New York, NY 18 Jun 1868 unm.

33 vii. Richard Valentine MORRIS[3], b. New York, NY 22 Aug 1838 d. New York, NY 24 Mar 1850 unm.

34 viii. Henry Walton MORRIS[3], b. New York, NY 27 Oct 1839 d. Saratoga, NY 28 Jul 1876 unm.

35 ix. Arthur Rutherford MORRIS[3], b. New York, NY 4 Jun 1846 d. Yokohama, JAPAN 17 Dec 1912, unm.

29   Honora Smith MORRIS[3] (Martha Pyne Morris[2], John Pyne[1]) b. New York, NY 2 Sep 1831. She m. Francis J. BARRETTO 5 May 1852, the son of Francis Barretto, Jr. and Anna Maria Julia Coster, who was b. 1829. He died 9 Jan 1894. She died in New York, NY some time after 1895. They had issue:

+ 53   i. Gerard Morris BARRETTO[4], b. 11 Feb 1853 in New York, NY.

  54 ii. Anna Coster BARRETTO[4], b. New York, NY 2 Nov 1854; dsp New York, NY 28 Sep 1856

  55 iii. Francis J. BARRETTO[4], b. New York, NY 22 Mar 1857; d. 15 Aug 1879 unm.

  56 iv. Nora Pyne BARRETTO[4], b. 13 Jan 1860 dsp 2 Apr 1863

31   Mary Pyne MORRIS[3] (Martha Pyne Morris[2] John Pyne[1]) b. New York, NY, 3 May 1835. m. on 19 Dec 1854, Jonathan EDWARDS, son of Judge Ogden Edwards and Harriet (Penfield) Edwards, who was born in New York, NY on 6 Nov 1821. He was an 1840 graduate of Princeton University, and was later admitted to the New York Bar. He practiced law both in NY and in California, returning to New York, where in 1878 he was the President of the Equitable Trust Company.

She died in Morristown, NJ on 27 Apr 1857, only 11 days after giving birth to their 2nd child. He m (2nd) Mary J. Jay on 5 Jun 1861, but no issue is reported from this marriage. He d. in New York City on 30 May 1882. Jonathan Edwards and Mary Pyne Morris Edwards had issue as follows:

57 i. Gerard Morris EDWARDS[4], b. 2 Jan 1856 in New York, NY; d. Nice, France 1 Mar 1900 unm. and is buried in the English Cemetery there.

+   58 ii. Mary Morris EDWARDS[4], b. 16 Apr 1857 in New York, NY.

53   Gerard Morris BARRETTO[4], (Honora Smith Morris[3], Martha Pyne Morris[2], John Pyne[1]) b. New York, NY 11 Feb 1853. He m. Laura Brevoort, daughter of Henry Brevoort and his wife Bridget on 4 Oct 1876 at Millburn, Essex County, NJ (2). She was b. in Boston, MA on 23 Nov 1853, one of a set of triplets. He died before 1900, she was still alive in Larchmont, Westchester County, NY in 1900 (3).

Gerard Morris Barretto and Laura Brevoort had issue as follows (3):

69   i. Gerard Morris BARRETTO[5], b. NJ 1878 unm.

70 ii. Francis BARRETTO[5], b. NY 1880 d. 14 Jan 1942 in NYC unm.

71 iii. Honora Bervoort BARRETTO[5], b. NY 1881; dsp 1885

72 iv. Arthur Rutherford BARRETTO[5], b. NY 1883, unm.

73   v. Helen BARRETTO[5], b. NY 1887 dsp before 1900

74 vi. Laurence Brevoort BARRETTO[5], He was b. 30 May 1890 in Larchmont, NY. He was educated in private schools in Hoosick, NY, then worked for the Plainfield, NJ newspaper and a Wall Street publishing house. During World War I, "Larry", as he came to be called, was a volunteer ambulance driver for the American Field Service (AFS) in both France and Belgium, for which service he was awarded the Croix de Guerre.

In WWII he was an enlistment officer for the AFS and later a war correspondent in the China-Burma-India theater.

He was a well known novelist, writing several works from 1925 through 1947. For much of this time he lived in New York City, moving to Carmel, California before 1955.

He m. Anna Appleton Flichtner on 20 Oct 1923. He was DSDI # 483. He d. at Carmel, California on 30 Dec 1971 (4), without issue.

75 vii. Phyllis BARRETTO[5], b. NY 1892, m. Kerr Eby, son of Rev Charles S. Eby and Eilen Keppel, b. in Tokyo, JAPAN 1889 at Greenwich, CT on 5 Jun 1935 (5). He d. 18 Nov 1946 at Norwalk, CT. She d. without issue.

CHART of the DESCENDANTS of HONORA SMITH MORRIS

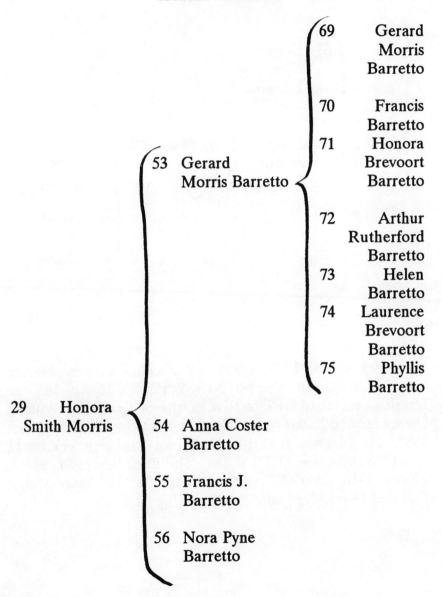

69   Gerard Morris Barretto

70   Francis Barretto

71   Honora Brevoort Barretto

53 Gerard Morris Barretto

72   Arthur Rutherford Barretto

73   Helen Barretto

74   Laurence Brevoort Barretto

75   Phyllis Barretto

29   Honora Smith Morris

54 Anna Coster Barretto

55 Francis J. Barretto

56 Nora Pyne Barretto

159

CHART of DESCENDANTS of MARY PYNE MORRIS

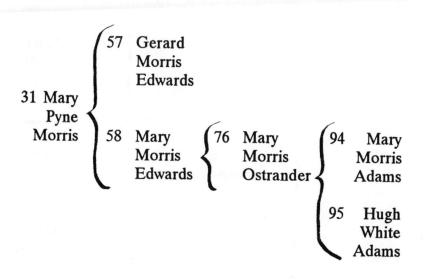

58   Mary Morris EDWARDS[4] (Mary Pyne Morris[3] Martha Pyne Morris[2], John Pyne[1]) b. New York, NY 16 Apr 1857 m. Charles Ferdinand OSTRANDER, son of Ferdinand William Ostrander and Sarah Ann Wright, in Brooklyn, NY on 11 Oct 1887. He who was b. in King's County, Brooklyn, NY on 11 Oct 1856. She was DSDI # 374. She d. 22 Sep 1930. He d. 27 Apr 1916. Charles Ferdinand Ostrander and Mary Morris Edwards Ostrander had a daughter (Fig 62):

Fig 62 The Ostrander Family, 1906
Charles F. Ostrander   M. M. Ostrander   M. M. Edwards Ostrander

161

+ 76 i. Mary Morris OSTRANDER[5] (Fig 64), (Mary Morris
        Edwards[4], Mary Pyne Morris[3], Martha Pyne Morris[2], John
        Pyne[1]) b. Manhattan, New York, NY 17 Sep 1888, m. Hugh
        White ADAMS, Jr. (Fig 65) on 1 Jun 1922 at St.
        Bartholomew's Church in Manhattan, NY (6). He attended
        Harvard University and studied in Europe before entering
        law school at Columbia University from which he graduated
        in 1900. He was the son of MAJ Hugh White Adams, a
        young officer of the Union Army who was promoted for
        bravery in 1863 and d. 7 May 1916 in Yonkers, NY, and
        Caroline Barker Haywood, b.28 May 1876 at Peekskill,
        Putnam Co, NY. Mary Morris Ostrander Adams d. in 29
        Sep 1955 in NYC and is buried in Woodlawn Cemetery.
        She was DSDI # 448. Hugh White Adams, Jr d. 5 Dec 1938
        in NYC. They had issue (Fig 63) as follows (7):

+ 94 i. Mary Morris ADAMS[6], b. 5 Apr 1923 in New York, NY.

  95 ii. Hugh White ADAMS III[6], 15 Feb 1925 in New York,
        NY. He was in the Ordinance Company of the 24th Infantry
        Division and served during WWII. He went on to Princeton
        University where he took a B.A. Degree in 1948. He was an
        Economist in the Office of Economic Development in
        Newark, NJ. He m. Anne Mechelina Scheerder in NYC on
        26 Jan 1957. There are no children of this marriage.

Fig 63   The Adams Family, 1929
Hugh White Adams, Jr.   Mary Morris Ostrander Adams
Hugh White Adams,III   Mary Morris Adams

163

Fig 64 Mary Morris Ostrander Adams, 1939

Fig 65 Hugh White Adams, Jr., 1924

165

94 Mary Morris ADAMS[c], (Mary Morris Ostrander[r], Mary Morris Edwards[4], Mary Pyne Morris[3], Martha Pyne Morris[2], John Pyne[1]) b. NYC 5 Apr 1923. She m. LT. Bernard Walter Clarke ROBERTS, RNVR on 29 Jul 1945 at Christ Church, TRINIDAD. He was b. 1 Jun 1906 in ENGLAND. They lived in various parts of the British Commonwealth during his duties as a Managing Director of Oldhams Press. He d. 4 Mar 1976 in Epsom, Surrey, ENGLAND. She resides in England. They had issue as follows:

+ 127 i. Nesta Anne ROBERTS[7] (Fig 66), (Mary Morris Adams[6], Mary Morris Ostrander[5], Mary Morris Edwards[4], Mary Pyne Morris[3], Martha Pyne Morris[2], John Pyne[1]) b. 23 Feb 1947 in Three Bridges, Sussex, ENGLAND. She m. (1st) David William WAY on 9 Oct 1969 at Kingswood Church, Surrey. They were divorced in England, but had issue (Fig 67):

147 i. Sally-Anne WAY[8], b. 27 Jul 1971 in Durban, SOUTH AFRICA.

148 ii. Amanda Jane WAY[8], b. 14 Jun 1973 in Johanesburg, SOUTH AFRICA.

She m. (2nd) Ian William PARKER (Fig 66) on 5 Dec 1980 and they have issue (Fig 67):

149 iii. Thomas Ian William PARKER[8], b. 23 Oct 1982 in Yeovil, Somerset, ENGLAND.

150 iv. Jenny Lynne PARKER[8], b. 6 Sep 1985 in Yeovil, Somerset, ENGLAND.

+ 128 ii. Allan Bernard ROBERTS[7] (Fig 66), (Mary Morris Adams[6], Mary Morris Ostrander[5], Mary Morris Edwards[4], Mary Pyne Morris[3], Martha Pyne Morris[2], John Pyne[1]) b. 21 Feb 1949 in Durban, SOUTH AFRICA. He attended the London College of Printing and is currently a Director of a Printing Company in Sussex. He m. Nichola Middleton on 17 Jul 1989 at the Lewes Registry Office, East Sussex, and they have issue:

151 i. Joshua Allan ROBERTS[8], b. 12 Jul 1990 in Cuckfield, Sussex, ENGLAND.

*Fig 66 The Roberts Children and Son-in-Law, Dec 1987
Allan Roberts Nesta Anne Parker Ian William Parker*

*Fig 67 Four Mary Morris Adams Roberts Grandchildren, Dec 1987
Sally-Anne Way   Amanda Jane Way   Thomas Parker
Jenny Parker*

168

CHART of DESCENDANTS of MARY MORRIS ADAMS

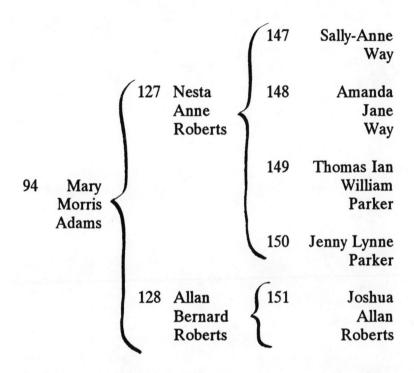

		147	Sally-Anne Way
	127 Nesta Anne Roberts	148	Amanda Jane Way
94 Mary Morris Adams		149	Thomas Ian William Parker
		150	Jenny Lynne Parker
	128 Allan Bernard Roberts	151	Joshua Allan Roberts

(1) Leach Papers, vol VII, p1835
(2) Index to NJ Marriages, Vol B-R, p.242
(3) 1900 Federal Census: Larchmont, Mamaroneck Twp., Westchester
    County, NY
(4) New York Times 2 Jan 1972, p.55, col. 1
(5) New York Times 6 Jun 1935, p19, col. 1
(6) Bride Index, Manhattan, NY #14551
(7) 1925 NY State Census, Manhattan

NOTES

170

AFTERWORD

Well, gentle reader, there you have it! An interesting lot, as set forth in the preface. It would have been quite beyond the scope of this study of a family history to bring in all the backgrounds and pedigrees of the female lines as they became connected to the family by marriage. In the Pyne line there were many New York pedigrees and in the Bankhead line many Virginia and Pennsylvania pedigrees. All the Pyne women married into prominent families. It should be noted that the Pyne men married well, especially the three generations from Smith Pyne to his grandson Frederick Glover Pyne.

The male line marriages brought into the family lineal descent from William Floyd a New York Signer of the Declaration of Independence. They also brought in lineal descent from General Philip Schuyler, General James Clinton, New York Governor DeWitt Clinton, Sir Thomas Fitch (Baron by Patent #905), COL Henry Moore, the Crugers, Van Rensselaers, Crosbys, Clarksons, and many others of great fame and service to country and (earlier) to King.

The female line marriages brought into the family descent from other Signers including Lewis Morris, Robert Morris, Philip Livingston; and Mayflower and Puritan connections to Allerton, Cushman, Biddle, Hall; as well as many other important colonial families such as Nixon, White, and Lytle.

The family was a dutiful and conservative lot of people. Believing strongly in the right of expression and of the absolute need for education, they supported the American Revolution. The family have had very many representatives in the Services and among the Clergy, because that is a function of their view of responsibility.

It should not come as a surprise to us that persons of learned upbringing and cultivated turns of mind would come to know each other. That is still true today. How much was it true 200 years ago! There were no Holiday Inns, no Interstate Highways to wisk one from place to place; you stayed where your parents had friends, relatives, or acquaintances. And you stayed not just for supper or the weekend; you stayed for weeks or even months! The children got to know each other; and surprise, they married! So your grandchilden or great-grandchildren carry the genes of all their progenitors back through the decades and centuries, and it is no wonder that there should be some relationship of a cousinly nature.

The author prays that some future researcher will carry on this work. Please make corrections as better information becomes available, add new data, refine old material, rewrite, shine, and polish. But mostly, he prays that the new writer will pass it on!

Any of you who read this study of an immigrant from Ireland, seeking fame and fortune in the new land and braving dangers and difficulties we can hardly imagine; consider the hardships to be overcome, the lengthy and less than comfortable ocean passage, the unkown disease hazards, and the frightful relative cost of everything. Then try to emulate and preserve the same traits in your own family.

Please, those of you that are encouraged, tempted, pressed by this humble work to do something for your own family-do so! You are the key, you are the one with the current information, with the knowledge of who and what, and with the memory of events and people. Do it before it is gone and forgotten, or before you are gone! If you do not do it, it will not get done. And that would be a tragic loss to all future generations down your line.

All errors, mistakes, misjudgements, and omissions are the full and sole responsibility of the writer. It is earnestly requested that any reader or researcher who finds or knows of any more complete data will be kind enough to furnish it for future editions.

APPENDIX

Several abbreviations used in the text of this family history may require explanation for the reader.

b. = birth, usually including date and place where known

bp. = baptisim with date and place

c. = circa. About, approximate date where a more specific date is not known or given in reference

d. = died, with date and place where known

dsp = decessit sine prole; died without issue

DAR= The National Society of the Daughters of the American Revolution. Founded 1890. Open to any women who is descended from a contributor to the cause of American Independence.

DSDI = Descendants of the Declaration of Independence. Founded in 1907. Open only to direct lineal descendants of a signer.

GSCW = General Society of Colonial Wars. Founded in 1893. Open to all male lineal descendants of persons who served in a military or civil capacity during any of the wars in which the American Colonies were engaged between the settlement of Jamestown (13 May 1607) and the Battle of Lexington (19 Apr 1775).

MOLLUS = Military Order of the Loyal Legion of the United States. Founded on 15 April 1865, the day of President Lincoln's death. Open to all male lineal descendants of Commissioned Officers who served in the Union Forces during the Civil War.

SAR= The National Society of the Sons of the American Revolution. Founded 1889. Open to male lineal descendants of continental or state military or patriot contributors to the cause of independence.

SR = The General Society Sons of the Revolution. Founded 1876. Open to male lineal descendants of military or civil bodies that assisted in the establishment of American Independence.

In some of the early generations, a reader will come across a date written, for example, as 1563/64. That is not the author's whim in not knowing which of two years to choose, but a requirement of good genealogical reporting. It comes about because of the calendar.

There is a difference between the ecclesiastical and the historical calendars. The first is called the Julian, the second the Gregorian. From the time of the Council of Nicea in 325 AD, the calendar was the Julian or ecclesiastical one, that used the Feast of the Annunciation, which falls on 25 March, as the New Year's Day. In the course of the next 1200 years, it was also found that the calendar was getting behind the solar year. This was corrected in 1582 by adding the 10 needed days, and making the New Year begin on 1 Jan.

Not all countries accepted this arrangement, until the year 1752, when 11 days where added on 3 Sep of that year. However, the time between 1 Jan and 25 Mar in years before 1752 need to be reported in double dates because many clerks were still using the older system.

176

DISCUSSION of the DESCENT from HERBERT de PYN of UPTON PYNE (1154)

to

JOHN PYNE of EAST DOWN (1564)

I HERBERT de PYN I was a member of and an important part of the ancient French Aquitaine House of de Pins (Precis Generale de la Maison de Pins). He came to England with Queen Eleanor, wife of Henry II in 1154. He was a witness to a deed c. 1160 (Patent Rolls); and d. 1166 (Black and Red Books of the Exchequer), leaving 4 sons, the eldest of whom was Sir Simon de Pyn.

II SIMON de PYN, b. in Aquitaine, is listed as holding a Knight's fee in 1166 (Red Book of the Exchequer, Vol 1, P. 251). He is reported as bearing the ancient arms of the Pyne family (Risdon's Note Book of Devon, p 203). He left issue, inter alia, a son, Sir Herbert de Pyn.

III HERBERT de PYN II must have been b. in Devon c. 1165. He was granted additional Manors by King John in 1216 (Polwhele's History of Devonshire, Vol 1, p 267). He was succeeded in his holdings as Lord of the Manors by his son Sir Herbert de Pyn.

IV HERBERT de PYN III, Lord of the Manors of Upton Pyne, Bramford Pyne, Washford Pyne, Colum Pyne, and others in Devon (Tax Rolls for Devon) and Cornwall was b. in Devon c. 1191. He was a loyal Knight in the reign of King Henry III. He may have d. c. 1247. He left his son, Simon de Pyn, as heir.

V SIMON de PYN II, was b. in Devon c. 1218. Possibly killed at the Battle of Lewes 14 May 1264, leaving issue, his son Sir Herbert de Pyn.

VI HERBERT de PYN IV, b in Devon c. 1242, was presented as Patron of the Church at Upton Pyne on 12 Oct 1264 (Exeter Episcopal Registers), and appears in the Hundred Rolls of 1275 as Lord of the Manors of Upton Pyne and Bramford Pyne. He was Knighted before 1273 (Exeter Episcopal Records). He was summoned to fight against the Scots in 1301 by King Edward I (Writs of Parliament). He d. 1309, leaving 3 children including his eldest, John de Pyn.

VII JOHN de PYN, b. in Devon c. 1279, m. Margery de Saunford in 1308. He owned much land in both Devon and Cornwall(Rolls of Parliament), including the Manors of Upton Pyne and Bramford Pyne. He d. 1336, leaving two sons, the eldest being Sir Thomas de Pyne.

VIII THOMAS de PYNE, b. Devon c. 1309, was Knighted by King Edward III in 1328 (Risdon's "Survey of the County of Devon"). He succeeded to the manor of Washford Pyne and other fees held by his great-great-grandfather Sir Herbert de Pyn III, while his younger brother, William de Pyne, inherited Upton Pyne and Colum Pyne. He left two sons and a daughter and d. 1364.

IX OLIVER PYNE, eldest son of Thomas de Pyne, was b. in Devon c. 1342. He bore the ancient arms of his ancestors (Heralds Visitations). He m. Eleanor de Downe late in life (1396), and thus became possessed of the family estate of East Down in Devon (Prince's "The Worthies of Devon"). He left issue, Robert Pyne.

X ROBERT PYNE, son of Oliver Pyne and Eleanor de Downe of East Down and Ham in Morwenstow (Feudal Aids) was b. in Devon c. 1398. He m. Thomazine Ilcombe and had issue, John Pyne.

XI JOHN PYNE, son of Robert Pyne and Thomazine Ilcombe was b. in Devon c. 1431. He m. Joan Salle (Vivian's Devon Visitations, p 76). He was Lord of the Manors of East Down, Ham, and Washford Pyne. He d. in 1483, leaving 3 children: Nicholas Pyne of whom we treat, Thomas Pyne, and Alice Pyne.

XII NICHOLAS PYNE, eldest son of John Pyne and Joan Salle was b. in Devon c. 1456. He m. Thomazine Winslade. He was Lord of the Manor of East Down and owner or part-owner of many other lands in Devon and Cornwall (Proceedings in Chancery). He d. in 1510, leaving issue, inter alia, George Pyne, his 2nd son, 3rd child.

XIII GEORGE PYNE was b. in Devon c. 1487 and was executor of his father's will. He succeeded to the Manor of East Down and other Devon properties. The Manor of Ham went to his older brother Thomas. He m. c. 1505 Isabel Appleton. He d. in 1530 leaving 3 sons: Nicholas Pyne of whom we treat, Andrew Pyne, and Augustine Pyne.

XIV NICHOLAS PYNE, eldest son of George Pyne and Isabel Appleton was b. at East Down, Devon in 1509. He was Lord of the Manor of East Down, and of many other properties in Devon. He m. Elizabeth Chichester and had issue. In 1564, William Hervy, Clarenceux King of Arms, made a Visitation of Devon at East Down for Nicholas Pyne that included their son John. He d. in 1574, after his only son John Pyne, of whom we treat.

XV JOHN PYNE, only son of Nicholas Pyne and Elizabeth Chichester, was b. at East Down, Devon c. 1533. He married Honor Penfound. A pedigree from a Visitation of the College of Arms was recorded for him in 1564 (Coll Arms D7 73).

180

DISCUSSION of the DESCENT from JOHN PYNE of EAST DOWN and HONOR PENFOUND (1564)

to

FREDERICK WALLACE PYNE (1992)

XV JOHN PYNE, the only son of Nicholas Pyne and Elizabeth Chichester was b. at East Down, Devon c. 1533. He married Honor Penfound. A pedigree from a Visitation of the College of Arms was recorded for him in 1564 (Coll Arms D7 73). He d. in 1572. He and his wife Honor Penfound had 6 sons and 4 daughters (Parish Reisters of Devon, Dorset, and Somerset). The 3rd son, George, was the progenitor of the line that included Thomas Pyne, who came to New York in 1828, and was the grandfather of Moses Taylor Pyne (as noted in Chapter IV). It is the 4th son, John Pyne, however, of whom we treat.

XVI JOHN PYNE, bp. 16 Jan 1563/64 at East Down, took a B.A. degree from Cambridge Hall, Cambridge in 1585 and was ordained into Holy Orders in 1587 as the Rector of East Down. He was buried there on 21 Feb 1615/16 (Devon Wills and Administrations).

This John Pyne (1564-1616), was married and left 2 sons and 2 daughters. His will was admitted to probate on 7 Sep 1616. (Wills in the Consistory Court of the Bishop of Exeter and Somerset House Wills) The Rev John Pyne's second son was Josias Pyne.

XVII JOSIAS PYNE was was bp 29 Nov 1604 and married Christian, daughter of Philip Heydon at Arlington on 21 Jun 1626. (Star Chamber Proceedings Book 28 No. 2, A.D. 1690; Arlington Parish Register). Josias Pyne had a son, Philip Pyne.

XVII PHILIP PYNE was bp. at Arlington on 2 Feb 1626/27 and d. Nov 1690. He m. by license of 12 Nov 1644 (1st) Anne widow of James Oxenham (Chancery Proceedings, Charles I. Bundle 26 No. 6, Stevens vs Pyne; Exeter Marriage Licenses) Philip and Anne Pyne had 5 children, the youngest son being John Pyne, of whom we treat.

XIX JOHN PYNE was bp. at West Down on 30 May 1655. He went to Exeter College and St. Alban's Hall, Oxford, from which he graduated B.A. in 1676 and was ordained and became the Vicar of the parish at Yarnescombe (Alumni Oxonsienses; Index Ecclesiasticus). He m. by license of 7 Feb 1681/82 Joan Hunt and had issue, the 4th child being Cornelius Pyne (Exeter Marriage Licenses). He d. there in May 1723 and is buried in the churchyard, as is his wife who had d. in Nov 1712. (Yarnescombe Parish Register)

XX CORNELIUS PYNE, the 4th child of The Rev John Pyne of Yarnescombe is reported to have been bp. on 10 Nov 1687, although this writer believes that to be an error of the copiest, since he was age 19 when admitted to Trinity College, Dublin on 2 Jun 1708. The date of this christening was much more likely to have been 10 Nov 1689 (Yarnescombe Parish Register). He took his B.A. in 1712 and an M.A. in 1715 (Alum. Dub.). He was ordained into Holy Orders and was Vicar of Kilworth from 1719 to his death in 1749. He m. by license Margaret, widow of Hugh Crosse on 6 May 1732. Their only child was a son, John Pyne.

XXI JOHN PYNE of Kilworth (Ballinacarriga), the only child of The Rev Cornelius Pyne, was b. c. 1735. He m. by license Isabella Pyne in 1757 and had issue (Cloyne Marriage License Bonds). The children of this marriage consisted of 3 sons and 2 daughters, of whom the 2nd son was John Pyne.

XXII JOHN PYNE, the 2nd son of John and Isabella Pyne was born in Nenagh, County Tipperary, Ireland on 14 Feb 1766. He m. c. 1789 Honora Smith, daughter of O'Brien Smith and Margaret Parsons. There were eight children by this marriage; 3 sons and 5 daughters. One of the young sons died in Ireland in 1805. John and Honora Pyne removed to Charleston, South Carolina with their five daughters and two remaining sons, O'Brien and Smith Pyne, where they arrived on 28 Feb 1808. He d. on 13 Jun 1813 and is buried in St. Michael's churchyard in Charleston. She died in Newport, Rhode Island on 21 Aug 1835.

XXIII SMITH PYNE, only surviving son of John and Honora Pyne, was b. in Bloomfield Lodge, Nenagh, County Tipperary, Ireland on 9 Jan 1803. He was educated at Eton College, took his B.A. from Columbia in 1823 and an M.A. in 1827. He was ordained into Holy Orders and had a most distinguished career. He m. Emma Francis Rogers in New York on 23 May 1825 and had issue, among whom, their 3rd son was Charles March Pyne. Smith Pyne d. 7 Dec 1875 and is buried in New York. (See also Chapter VI).

XXIV CHARLES MARCH PYNE, the 3rd, and youngest, son of Smith and Emma Pyne was b. 27 Feb 1839 in Jersey City, NJ. He took a B.A. Degree from St. James College in 1858. After serving in the American Civil War, he then studied for Holy Orders at Berkley Divinity School and was ordained. He m. Eliza Glover in Middletown, CT on 12 Nov 1873 and they had issue, inter alia, John Frederick Glover Pyne, who as an adult dropped the "John" and became known as Frederick Glover Pyne. Charles March Pyne d. 4 Feb 1892 and is buried in Arlington National Cemetery. (See also Chapter X).

XXV   FREDERICK GLOVER PYNE was b. 5 Jun 1879 in Central Falls, RI.   He was a naval officer, retiring with the rank of RADM.   He m. Ellen Roosevelt Jones in Elizabeth, NJ on 23 Sep 1901. They had 3 sons, the eldest of whom was Frederick Cruger Pyne. (Burke's Landed Gentry, 1939 ed. p 2875) RADM   Pyne died 15 Apr 1962 and is buried in Arlington National Cemetery. (See also Chapter XI).

XVI FREDERICK CRUGER PYNE was b. 8 Sep 1902 on the Island of Guam. He was a 1924 graduate of the United States Military Academy at West Point, NY, served in the Army (LTC) and with private industry as an Engineer.   He   m. Helen Louise Wallace in Washington, DC on 25 Apr 1925. They had three children, the eldest of whom is Frederick Wallace Pyne. LTC Pyne d. 19 Dec 1984 and is buried in Arlington National Cemetery. (See also Chapter XI).

XXVII FREDERICK WALLACE PYNE was b. 19 Aug 1926 in El Paso, TX. He took a B.S. Degree from Tri-State College, Angola, IN, and an M.S. from Johns Hopkins University. He is a Professional Engineer, a Fellow of the American Society of Civil Engineers, and a Professor of Mathematics. He m. Jo Ann Rammes (nee Donelda Jane Bennett), adopted daughter of Jack Albert Rammes at Birmingham, MI on 18 Jul 1952 and has issue. (See also Chapter XII).

NOTES

186

BIBLIOGRAHY

This bibliographic essay is designed to assist the reader, not only in finding some of the material cited in the body of the text of this book, but also in discovering other resources used in its preparation. It is also hoped that a reader may be led into using some of these works in the writing of his own genealogical article or book.

Barnes, Donald R., and Lackey, Richard S.; "Write It Right", Lyon Press, 1983. A small paperback book of immense practical value. Discusses purpose and focus. Gives specific and practical help on matters of numbering systems, organization of genealogical work, citations, and arrangement.

Census, US. No Genealogist worth his salt can function long without recourse at some time in his research to the schedules of the United States Census. In preparation of this book, in particular, it became necessary to use the 1810 and 1820 records of Charleston, SC, and others of New York, including the 1925 New York State Census. The early US censuses asked for head of Household, and for numbers of males and females by age cohorts, as well as for free colored persons, slaves, foreigners, and others (usually by the same age cohorts). Thus, if one knows the makeup of a family, it is possible to identify that family, and even individuals within that family by judicious use of the Census Records.

187

Charleston, SC Papers. During the period 1808-1824, in which the author was most interested, there were three newspapers in Charleston: The Charleston Courier, The Charleston Gazette, and The Charleston Times. The first was a daily, except Sunday, paper that was largely commercial. It would, therefore, be the best place in which to find information on the arrival and departure of shipping. The Library of Congress does not have a complete run of this paper, and no index has yet been prepared. The Charleston County Library does have such a run, but searching is very laborious and has not yielded any results regarding the name of the vessel on which John Pyne arrived. The other papers in Charleston at this time were also dailies, but tended to cater more to news items, including that from other places, national news, and social news. It is the social news in which we are interested. Notices of deaths, weddings, and social events were reported promptly. Much of this has been extracted and collected together in the South Carolina Historical and Genealogical Magazine.

Falley, Margaret D., "Ancestral Research, Irish and Scotch-Irish", GPC, Baltimore, Md, 1988. This 2-volume work is by far the finest source book on the Irish Genealogical area the author has come across. It is full of data on printed works, Family Histories, Library holdings, parish, town, and county records.

Family History Library, Salt Lake City. This is the largest and the finest Genealogical Library in the World! If one has an opportunity to go there, it is not to be missed. But you cannot just walk in and ask for the answers to your genealogical questions. You must do the work. People are available to help you, but you have to be prepared with enough data to research what you need. Fortunately, much of this help is also available to you on a local basis. Many Church of Jesus Christ of Latter Day Saints (LDS) buildings will house a local Family History Center. At such a Center you will be able to access a great deal of data stored on Microfiche, Compact Disk, or Microfilm. If you know name, location, date, or parents you will probably be able to obtain a lead on the genealogical question to which you seek an answer. This answer may not be a direct solution to the problem, but in the form of a number for a microfilm, stored at Salt Lake City, that can be ordered for you at a small fee, for delivery to the local Center you have been visiting. When it arrives you use it just as though you were in the Library at Salt Lake City! With practice and persistence you will become experienced in the use of this magificant resource. It can then be a vehicle by which you can resolve many of your genealogical difficulties.

Greenwood, Val D.; "The Researcher's Guide to American Genealogy", 2nd Edition, GPC, 1990. This is a standard all-purpose reference work. Used as a text in many genealogical courses, it is both comprehensive and instructive.

189

Hereditary Register of the United States of America. An annual publication valuable because it includes in one place a list of, and requirements for, entry into the various Hereditary Societies It also has a list of Family Societies.

Irish Genealogist, The, "The Pynes of County Cork", Part IV, 1987 by Dr. Henry F. Morris. This is a five part genealogical essay on all of the Irish Pynes from the Upton Pyne and East Down Lines as well as others that Morris could not connect with them. Dr. Morris did an extensive amount of research into the Irish and English genealogical material. He was partly aided in this effort by Col. Anthony Masters Pyne, whom the author had met in Bruges in 1976. It is Part IV of the Morris work (pp 235-239) that is of particular value to the descendants of The Rev. Cornelius Pyne of Kilworth, because the information it contains pins down his marriage and the birth of his son and his grandchildren. This allows the definitive connection that was so long missing in the family history. The Irish Genealogist is the Journal of the Irish Genealogical Research Society whose headquarters are now in the Challoner Club, Pont Street, London SWIX OBG. The Society was formed in the office of York Herald in the College of Arms, London on 15 Sep 1936, the first issue of the Journal appearing in 1937.

Jordan, Wilfred, Ed."Colonial and Revolutionary Families of Pennsylvania", Lewis Historical Publishing Company, New York,1935. It is the Newhall Family compilation part of this work that is of special interest to the reader of this book.

190

Land   Records.   One of the strongest drawing cards that brought people from their old homes in other countries to America   was the opportunity for land ownership. The acts of dividing, describing, marking, and recording individual parcels of land became one of the most important activities of government. Land ownership created the hope for the future. Therefore all things relating to such ownership were seen as critical to the people.   They would tolerate no delay in the process that marked, conveyed, and recorded land transfers. Very many of the early prominent persons in this country had been surveyors.   Along the Eastern Seaboard States, the old English method of metes and bounds surveying was, and still is, used. The land to be conveyed from one party to another was physically marked on the ground and measured by a surveyor. He then prepared a description of the bounds of the parcel, including its area. This was incorporated into a deed to be signed by the person granting (or selling) the land. The signed and sealed deed was then copied by a clerk into a book, kept especially for this purpose. A court house was erected in which to house this book, and others like it. The books were indexed, and this became a permanent record of all Land transfers in the area covered by that Court House.   The process still continues today, in the same way. The value to the genealogist of these Land Records is that they reveal names, dates, places, and costs. Coupled with other data in the Court House, such as Wills, Marriage Licenses, Law and Equity Cases, a rather full picture of a person being researched unfolds.

Mountain, William D.; "The March Family". This is a projected 8 vol. work by a genealogist whose efforts this author found to be quite complete and well referenced. It is a full genealogy of this important family, connected by marriage to the Pynes.

New England Historic Genealogical Society. Organized in 1845, this is the oldest genealogical society in the world. A journal, called The Register, has been published since 1847. It has a lending Library and a sales department. If any of your ancestors came to New England or left from New England to head further west in the 18th or 19th century, you may find this society of special interest.

New York Genealogical and Biographical Society. This Society was founded in 1869. It has published The Record since 1870. This is one of the leading genealogical journals in America. A very great deal of biographical and historical information is to be found in these volumes. It contains enormous amounts of information about New York families as well as families from nearby states such as New Jersey, Pennsylvania, and the New England States.

New York Times. This paper began publication in 1851, and has produced a daily paper ever since. For genealogical purposes it can be invaluable. There are a series of Indexes that list subjects, people, and places. They are an aid to the particular dated paper and page number of the indexed item. In addition, there is a Personal Name Index to the New York Times that is a much faster route to information about persons. Deaths in this paper are noted both by obituaries, if the importance of the person suggested an article, and by short notice. The latter has not been indexed. The obituaries are collected in separate volumes, and indexed.

Pelling, George; "Beginning Your Family History in Great Britian", GPC, 1989. A small, paperback little jewel of a book. Leads one to Foster's Oxford Alumni; Venn's Cambridge Alumni; the Phillimore Atlas; Gibson's Guides; and innumerable other sources with their location and the information to be found in them.

Pyne, Moses Taylor; "Descendants of Galceran dePinos", NY 1915. This is an extensive and broad work of the earliest roots of the Pyne family. Many very early records in Spain, France, and England were searched and the information extracted. The format was then to number each of the sources by grouping them into a Spanish House, two French Houses, and the English House. For each of these "Houses", a multi-page Pedigree was made, using the numbered references as required. Thus a very great deal of information is conveyed in a simple, graphic approach. A copy of this book is in The Family History Library in Salt Lake City, as is a microfilm print that may be ordered through a local LDS Family History Center (Film 1125102-item #14).

Pyne, Moses Taylor: "Memorials of the Pyne Family, Vol. 1", Princeton 1919. Although this work is titled "Vol. 1", no additional volumes were ever prepared. Following his earlier work on the origins and very early records of the family, Moses Taylor Pyne launched himself upon a massive exposition of the whole family genealogical record. It was too much. He never got beyond "Vol. 1", although it alone is a very important work. Because it was privately copied and bound, not published as was his 1915 work, there are very few copies of this critical Pyne family history available. Much of his information is especially valuable as regards the Pynes in Ireland, since his work was all done before the disastrous fire that burnt so many of the Irish Records in Dublin in 1922 during the "troubles". Available as Film 1559419-item #1 from the FHL.

Rubincam, Milton, Ed.; "Genealogical Research: Methods and Sources", Washington, DC, 1980. This is Vol I of a two volume work by the American Society of Genealogists.

Smith, Frank;"Genealogical Gazetteer of England", GPC, 1987. An alphabetical dictionary and locator of places in England, including old parishes, giving the date of the earliest entry in their registers. An indispensable reference tool for those searching for people who were born, baptized, married, or interred in ancient parish churches in England.

Social Register. A useful resource for the genealogist because it will frequently list children, education, position, and clubs or hereditary societies to which a listed subscriber belongs. Originally published annually by city, since 1977 in one comprehensive volume. Sometimes referred to as the "Black Book" because of its color and to distinguish it from other Social Lists with different color bindings. A full run is found in the Library of Congress.

Underwood, Betty;"An Introduction to Genealogical Research". A very useful little paperback loaded with excellent information on all aspects of a genealogical project. Whether you wish to prepare a small article or a full family history and genealogical record as a book, this will prove helpful.

Virginia Families, Genealogies of, from the William and Mary College Quarterly, GPC, 1982. This five vol. work contains all the family history articles published in the Quarterly from its beginning in 1892 up until 1943. This includes nearly 500 genealogies. While only the entry for the Bankhead Family was used for this book, the reader should know of the larger scope of this comprehensive collection of Virginia Genealogies.

Visitation. The use of Coats of Arms sprang up in order to identify a particular Knight or Overlord. Soldiers and followers would rally at the banner of an easily recognizable pennon. Later, the broad surface of the shield provided a satisfactory means of display. This became extended to other personal items such as seals, gates, mantels, and windows. One does not need a high lineage to be entitled to a Coat of Arms, but one does need to have inherited such a right by grant of its use from his ancestors. The method of this grant of use of the "Right to Bear Coat Armour" in England became a Visitation by the College of Arms. The College was incorporated in 1484. Royal Commissions were issued to visit and examine the pedigrees of Knights, Nobles, and others claiming a right to bear Arms. These Visitations first commenced in 1530. If, after exhaustive review,the Heralds of the College concluded that a right to bear Arms was legitimate, that fact would be recorded or registered in a special book kept for that purpose. The last Visitation Commission was issued in 1686. These Registrations of Arms were done by County. The original drafts of The Visitation of Devon in 1620 were housed in the British Museum. These manuscripts have now been published by the Harleian Society. In addition to the material available in England, the Pyne Arms is also to be found in The Family History Library in Salt Lake City with the Harleian Society works (942 B4h, vol.6, p. 231). A reader searching for his own possible Coat of Arms will find other volumes for the other Counties on the same shelf area.

196

INDEX

C

California, U of	83,148	Calvary Ch.	42,38,49,50
Camberling, Anne	91	Camberling, S.J.	91
Cambridge, MA	81,86	Camp Nifty	114
Campbell, Robert H.	63	Campbell, Sarah M.	63
Carmalt, Rachel P.	70	Carmel, CA	158
Carroll County, MD	127,132	Carrollton, TX	138
Cary, Henry	38,53	Catonsville	132
Cazenovia, NY	108,114	Census, US	34
Central Falls, RI	104	Centreville, MD	71
Charlemagne, King	2	Charleston, SC	29,33,34,38,49,50,55,58
Charlotte, VT	84	Cherry Point, NC	132
Chesapeake College	146	Cheshire, CT	70,79
Chichester, Eliz	10,16	Christ Church	42
Christ Church, TRIN	166	Church Street	55
Citizenship	28,35	Civil War	62,98
Clark, Mary	79	Claymont, DE	138
Cleveland, OH	74	Clipper Ships	27
Cloyne	19	Coaldale, PA	74
Colleton, Co. of	33,34,49	Colorado Sps, CO	71
Colum Pyne	5,16	Columbia, U of	41,161
Compton, VA	79	Confederate Army	59
Conn. College	76	Cooke, Bertha J.	75
Cornwall	5	Correia, C. L.	86
Correia, J. L.	86	Correia, J. T.	86
Correia, Marg.	86	Coster, Anna M.J.	155
Covington, KY	83	Cowley, Charles R.	150
Cowley, David M.	150	Cowley, James R.	150
Cox, Julia E.	77	Crosby, Josepha	109
Cross, David M.	137	Cross, James Oliver	137
Crosse, Hugh	20	Crow, Catherine L.	147
Crow, Karen E.	147	Crow, Richard W.	147
Crow, Robert S.	147	Crow, Stuart J.	146
Crow, William H.	146	Cruger, Ann Mary	100
Cuckfield, ENG	167		

D

Darien, CT	94	De la Vega, Marg.	83
De la Vega, Sandra	83	de los Pinos	1
de Pins	2,15	de Pyn, Herbert	3,4,5,15,16
de Pyn, John	6	de Pyn, Simon	4,5
de Pyne, Thomas	6	Declaration of Inep6ndence	44
Devon, ENG4,	6	Di Tudini, Oldofredi	50
DiGiacomo, C.S.	137	DiGiacomo,, J.C.	137
DiGiacomo, Joseph C.	136	DiGiacomo, V.C.	137
Dry, Judith E.	137	Dunharrow	3,108
Durban, SA	166		

E

F

G

H

199

M

O

P

T

U

V

W

Y